Spiritual Lighthouse:

THE DREAM DIARIES OF ANN MARIE RUBY

Ann Marie Ruby

To the Little Shop Library
Enjoy reading!
With love
Ann Marie Ruby

Sacred appreciation from my soul to the four sacred souls whom I but call my Angels in disguise. You have traveled with me through all the struggles, obstacles, and blessings of life. Without you, this book would remain within the pages of my dream diaries, hidden away from this world and only within my chest. Now with your support and encouragement, I have taken pen to paper and have published my dream diaries. All my blessings be upon you, as you travel through this journey of life. As per your wish, you four remain unknown to this world, love you eternally forever.

I call these four, as they know, "The Four."

TABLE OF CONTENTS

"What fills a plate is but the grace of The Lord up in the Heavens above. Contents are but chosen by the will of grace. Out of thousands of nights, I have but chosen the forty."

-Ann Marie Ruby

MESSAGE FROM THE AUTHOR

Personal Reflection

"Perception is but the perspective of the personal mind where individual stories take birth and all her messages become immortal as they travel time."

-Ann Marie Ruby

July 26, 2017

Dawn peaks through my bedroom windows, streaming in the first glitter of morning glory. The sun rises as the Puget Sound and the Olympic Mountains watch over my home, as if they were keeping an eye over me throughout the dark night. Reflections through the windows of time are but the union of the present, the past, and the future. I love watching the Earth, as she has been standing here throughout time. Even when life moves on, all this nature will be standing here, watching over me today and you tomorrow.

Windows are the doors of reflection throughout time. Memories are personal reflections throughout eternity. Even though time passes by us, memories remain within the present through the pages of history. Some stories are written throughout history. Yet, some are lost within the pages of history as they were never told, but now are being collected through word of mouth. Through the wheels of time and the memories of personal diaries, we receive the gifts of these very personal stories.

Even then at times, some stories we have proof of and some we don't have any proof of, but just the word of a stranger whom we have never seen or might never see or encounter. My soul cries out for these unknown people and their unknown stories that come and land upon our doors from an unknown witness through the pages of history.

A page out of a personal diary floats throughout time as she lands upon the shore and brings to us a very personal story of a stranger. Dried ink and worn out pages come and land upon our hands through the open windows of acceptance. Today, I have placed ink to paper as I gather personal pages of my dreams from my diaries.

My personal diary is very different as she was created through the pages of my dreamland, where time laid still even though my life moved on. This Earthly body, which I call a vehicle, has moved on with time. Yet, night after night, my dreams have taken me to a different level of spiritual awakening. I have taken these pages of my life as blessings and have tried to learn from them. I know not all gifts are appreciated or accepted, but I must accept and learn from this gift. Alone and lost I felt at the beginning, but I knew this is a gift I must share with the world.

The birth of my very personal dream diary had taken place within the torn pages of my notepads, where I had written my dreams until I was gifted with a brand-new iPhone in 2011. Technology had replaced my paper and pen as I started to gather all my dreams onto my personal phone. Today I share my dream journal with all of you.

After research, I found out that dreams have guided all throughout history and today even scientists in addition to religious scholars, philosophers, and historians, have all touched upon this subject. I knew I must be brave and must stop pretending that if I sat in the total back of the classroom, no one would notice me. I must stand up and share my story with all the strangers in this classroom around the world.

I am a single spiritual woman who believes in life and all of humanity. Today, I stand amongst the strangers and know within this group, I have a dear friend whom I but call an Angel in disguise. Never do I look at a stranger and think, "Oh but another stranger," for I know amongst all the strangers, Angels too walk. This is how I live my life. It is hard and at times, mounds of obstacles but appear in front of me. I know it is then I must repeat to myself, obstacles are just that, obstacles. As we cross them, they are but in the past and we have with us the learned lessons of life.

I live in Seattle, Washington. I love the nature. The weather, with her true glory, brings a sense of calmness and joy within my heart. The musical concert the weather but displays for us each and every day is a free concert where each one of us gets a front row seat. Clear skies over the Puget Sound with the mountain views, were this night's blessings. Mother Nature shares her blessings with all whom but accept her. Each day is a brand-new entry within my diary of life as I safely conceal these sweet songs of appreciation within my soul. Amongst all of this, I hear true love blooming. I hear a mother's sweet and tender love to calm her child. I hear a father's advice to his children reflecting throughout the times of life.

I sit watching nature through my bedroom windows. I know I have this sweet and sour feeling, the uncomfortable feeling of, "I must do it somehow. I must acquire the courage to just get it out on paper." I have my iPhone and laptop on my lap, and I have on my warm, cozy flannel pajamas as the reflections of my life flash back through my memories. I should get words out and just get these thoughts of my dreams out on the screen. I have been blessed to have so many miracles in my life, all through the blessed dreams, the holy dreams which I call guidance from the Heavens above.

When our mind and body but fall asleep, our soul still guides us throughout eternity. Our soul is immortal even though our body is but not. Dreams are our pathway to the unknown and unseen. Throughout time, dreams have guided us to the unknown mysteries of the universe. Faith-based religions, spirituality, and wisdom have taken birth, all guided by holy dreams. Dreams guided by our inner soul have also been analyzed by mystics and scientists including Edgar Cayce, Ian Stevenson, Carl Jung, and others.

Sometimes we have dreams that make no sense but in due time, we know why the dream was given to us. I have been fortunate to have dreams in my life which have guided me to awaken spiritually as I believe in the unknown blessings The Lord but bestows upon us every day.

I believe life is a journey where we have as companions, obstacles and blessings. The path has been given to all of us. It is what, where, and why we land upon the path that makes all of us unique individuals.

I believe in prayers as guidance and saving grace. As we seek, knock, and ask each day, the answers but land upon us. For me, dreams have been my saving grace. I have received blessings and sometimes even messages over which I stayed awake worrying.

The path is difficult and at times the answer or hope I sought had not come upon my door.

Although my dreams have been accurate, the blessed ones and the ones I feared also came upon my door. I have learned that the scary dreams were given as guidance to show how I could avoid troubled bridges and prevent the worst. Life is always a gift from The Creator. We are all but travelers. Throughout the stormy nights, we carry the blessings and guidance with us as our sacred saviors.

Throughout the sunny bright hours of our lives, may we hold on to the guidance and blessings of The Creator and always save our saving grace for the stormy nights. At all times, we must remember we are all but the judged, not The Judge. I have my personal dreams and I carry them upon my spiritual journey through life. I have had these dreams as my personal lighthouse guiding me through life.

I have awakened spiritually and know these dreams are pure miracles from The Creator. I have written in this book, in detail, only a few of my very personal dreams. I have tried to keep my personal life, my family, and my friends far away in a safety blanket at all times. Please respect my privacy and bless my inner wish as I consider all humans as my own family. My hope is that maybe someone out there will have faith in his or her dreams and be blessed and guided by them and know we are all the blessed creation of The One Creator. At all times, my dream diary is my personal perspective where I voice only my own dreams.

Follow your dreams, the ones that but appear to us during the time our body and soul but separate as we fall asleep. Keep a diary of all your dreams and know when we seek guidance from the Heavens above, we do receive the guidance, but it's our job to remember.

We have these dreams as a guide to help us personally and help all of whom but seek, ask, and knock. May my dreams help you all have faith in The Creator and know it matters not how you call your Creator or what name you call your Creator by. There is only one Creator and may we all have faith. Faith is what keeps all but going throughout time.

May my dreams guide you to a better self, and an awakened spiritual soul. Hold on to the hands of the person next to you and as each one of us holds each other's hands, may not a single life be lost or fall off this blessed journey of life, but walk hand in hand to the house of our Creator.

Today, I see dawn finally peeking through after a dark night. The skies have become clear and the ferries are all ready to cross passengers over through the Puget Sound. Life is but a blessing each day. May my dream diaries give all hope and the spiritual guidance to cross over all the obstacles of life.

Time is patient and has taught me to be patient like her. Time knows she must keep on walking. No matter what life brings upon us, time moves on for she is but the traveler of life.

I want to walk with all of you and travel upon this unknown, unseen path that we have landed upon at birth and must continue till our last breath. On this journey, may we have as our true friend, truth, justice, and honor always guiding us as I have my dreams, my visions, and gifts from the unknown as my partner of life. May my dreams and prophecies be there for you today and the future generations tomorrow as a true friend during your time on this Earth.

As time passes by, we the present must gift the future generation some words of wisdom to hold on to. I have decided to leave my words of wisdom through my books. All my books are spiritual inspirations from the miracles of life. The biggest miracles of my life came through my blessed dreams.

All my sacred friends, come on this trip with me as I share with you my very personal dreams. Through this memory lane, we will all travel within my dreams. Throughout this travel, please know these are my personal dreams and the details are all to the best of my recollection. May my dreams be a friend in the dark night, shining like the candles of hope for all of whom but need them.

I know when science and all the living proof of life cannot answer the questions or answer how this is possible, I call them miracles from the beyond. In the ocean of life, we all float like vessels trying to find shore. It is then, these miracles are found floating in the ocean like a lighthouse trying to guide all of whom but seek. My dream diaries are my Spiritual Lighthouse, guiding me throughout life from the unknown land, beyond human knowledge called the land of miracles.

Within this book, I have included the research of my dreams. As I had awakened after each dream, I always did extensive research and tried to find out the meaning, and the scientific and philosophical aspects of each dream. I have included in this book the results of my personal research. This research is my very own and to the best of my knowledge as today I make public my very sacred diary.

Walk with me through the pages of my dreams as I have always kept a complete note of all my dreams with the date and place, I had received them. May these pages guide you to another land, the land of miracles, and may they bring back upon each door, the complete faith in The Omnipotent. Whatever you may call The Lord, and in whichever language, there is but one Creator, and we are all but the creation. Always in my mind, I carry the words of Carl Jung, "We have forgotten the age-old fact that God speaks chiefly through dreams and visions" (*Man and His Symbols* 92).

Throughout my diary, I have kept my personal identity hidden. I have kept all information about my personal life private as much as possible, for I only want my dreams as guidance, a helping hand, for all of you whom have these personal dreams and struggles of life. The Lord gives us miracles each day as guidance from the Heavens above. May I be like the lighthouse in the lost ocean guiding all of whom seek, ask, and knock for help.

Based on my dreams, I have written my very special prayer book for all of whom need to recite prayers I but call songs, throughout the lonely nights. I have also written books of original, inspirational quotations, as my dreams have always guided me throughout this journey of life. Now, I give you my dream diaries. My dreams have inspired my previous six books and now I have the dream diaries that had started my journey of life as a sacred soul.

Dreams have come to me within my entire life. I have chosen out of thousands, the forty nights of dreams. They are not synchronized by date but by my personal discretion throughout the book. Each dream is individually complete. Hold my hands throughout these pages, as I walk you through my dreams, my personal reflection through the windows of my life. I call her, *Spiritual Lighthouse: The Dream Diaries of Ann Marie Ruby.*

LIGHTHOUSE OF MY LORD[1]

My Lord The Omnipotent,

Guide me and all of my ways.

May I be protected by Your truth my Lord

For my last breath is but upon me.

Help me my Lord

For I am but lost.

Show me the truth of the unknown

For all is but lost to this World my Lord.

Pull me up my Lord

For the cold, shivering, unknown death

Is but drowning my last lights.

All the lost religions from all around history

Are but claiming Your name my Lord.

May I not be lost amongst them

For I call upon You, my Lord.

May my Lord's Ark pick me up

From the cold dark night's ocean.

May my soul be guided even in this dark ocean

By The

LIGHTHOUSE OF

MY LORD.

---

[1] From my previous book of spiritual prayers, *Spiritual Songs: Letters From My Chest*

INTRODUCTION

Eternal Footprints Through Dreams

"Scientific, religious, and philosophical scholars have all traveled upon the same mystical path, inquiring why dreams are but the eternal reflection of time— past, present, and future."

-Ann Marie Ruby

October 1, 2017

Travel through this chapter with me as we walk across the memory lanes of history across Abrahamic religious, mythological, philosophical, and scientific views of dreams. As I share with the world my very personal dreams throughout the pages of this book, I now would like to leave some footprints of the historical aspects of dreams.

Edgar Cayce said in his well-known quotation, "Dreams are today's answers to tomorrow's questions." All over the world and throughout time, dreams have guided humans toward the unknown, unseen future, the lost past, and the ongoing present. From ancient mythology to Hinduism to the Abrahamic religions to science today, all have walked upon this mystical path of dreams. Carl Jung described dreams as, "the facts from which we must proceed" (*Memories, Dreams and Reflections* 171).

Science through various neurological tests of the brain waves and eye movements has theorized dreams are real. It is the individual contents of the dream that no one can prove but one's own self and the evidence of life that comes after the dream.

I also believe dreams are a sacred, spiritual journey of the unknown. Miracles happen within the faith of dreams. Messages are received within the magical world of dreams. My dreams have walked with me and have become a reality during the daylight as they came upon me through the mystical nights.

Let us walk through the tunnels of history to see what we know about dreams. I am not an expert, a historian, nor a scientist, but just a person who believes in dreams. Ancient civilizations such as the Egyptians are well-known to have relied heavily on dreams. The Egyptians had dream interpreters and seers who would see dreams. Now, we do know the Egyptian pharaohs had developed very advanced technologies. Yet, we still don't know how they had developed some of these technologies during those times.

The pyramids, the mummies, and much more to this day, we have no clue how they were accomplished. Maybe, just maybe, they had help from dreams. My question is why have we stopped believing in dreams when such an advanced civilization was so dependent on dreams? Maybe it's now time we believe in dreams again and all the mysteries will again be resolved through dreams. Let us keep walking throughout history.

Let us walk into Hinduism as this is the oldest known religion still being practiced to this day. Within this house, again we see dreams and how dreams have shaped the religion. In Hinduism, the Mandukya Upanishad outlines the different states of consciousness which include: the waking state, the dream state, deep sleep, and the pure consciousness ("Mandukya Upanishad – 12 Verses on AUM"). Dreams appear repeatedly within all the texts of Hinduism such as the Bhagavad Gita, the Puranas, and the Vedas.

Let us now walk through Judaism, the first Abrahamic religion. The Talmud, one of the main texts of Judaism, covers dreams extensively. Within the Babylonian Talmud, Rabbi Berekiah said, "A dream, though it be fulfilled in part, is never completely realised" ("Berakhot" 55a). It is clear from this passage that sometimes dreams are completed within much longer periods than we the humans assume.

The text goes further to explain in detail how it took twenty-two years for one dream of Joseph to be fulfilled. The Talmud goes over Joseph, who is mentioned in the Torah, Bible, and the Quran. Joseph is described as a dreamer and a dream interpreter by all the Abrahamic religions. The Lord gave messages of prophecy in Joseph's dreams to guide him and others. Not only did he see and interpret his own dreams, but he also interpreted dreams for others including the Pharaoh in the ancient Egyptian civilization.

So, dreams given from the Heavens above is a bridge between all religions. This proves also why I have had so many dreams, yet I have seen the fulfillment of only a part of my dreams and I wait to see what happens to the other parts of my dreams. I know all the questions are answered in due time, for I know dreams are miracles from the Heavens above.

Let us now take a journey through the Bible and see how the Bible guides us through dreams. In the Book of Genesis, we see Jacob's Ladder dream. Jacob "dreamed, and behold a ladder set up on the earth, and the top of it reached to heaven: and behold the angels of God ascending and descending on it. And, behold, the LORD stood above it [...]" (*King James Version*, Genesis 28:12-13). From this Biblical verse, we see how the unknown and unseen all but appear within our knowledge from the Heavens above through dreams. So powerful are dreams. We should never forget this dream also unites Islam, Christianity, and Judaism. For even though they have divided amongst themselves, all their texts within their Holy Books talk of these two dreams—one is Jacob's Ladder and the other one is the dream of Joseph.

According to the Bible and other religious texts, dreams will be given to humans as written in the following verse of the Bible:

> "And it shall come to pass afterward, that I will pour out my spirit upon all flesh; and your sons and your daughters shall prophesy, your old men shall dream dreams, your young men shall see visions: And also upon the servants and upon the handmaids in those days will I pour out my spirit. And I will shew wonders in the heavens and in the earth, blood, and fire, and pillars of smoke. The sun shall be turned into darkness, and the moon into blood, before the great and terrible day of the Lord come. And it shall come to pass, that whosoever shall call on the name of the Lord shall be delivered: for in mount Zion and in Jerusalem shall be deliverance, as the Lord hath said, and in the remnant whom the Lord shall call" (*King James Version*, Joel 2:28-32).

Walking through these religions throughout history, we see the powerful impact and significance of dreams. Now let us take a journey through Islam and see the Islamic view on dreams. "Dreams have often been seen as vehicles of divine communication in the lives of famous Muslims" ("Dreams"). The two main texts of Islam, the Quran and Hadith, both contain many details about dreams.

In the Sahih Bukhari collection of the Hadith, Abu Huraira narrated, "Allah's Apostle said, 'When the Day of Resurrection approaches, the dreams of a believer will hardly fail to come true, and a dream of a believer is one of forty-six parts of prophetism, and whatever belongs to prophetism can never be false'" (Al-Bukhari, Volume 9, Book 87, Number 144).

These faiths from beginning of time to even this day and age, basically talk about the same aspects and have written down, through the lane of history, the truth and facts of dreams. How important dreams are and were to each faith is not a mystery as all faiths stand side by side with the same basic values.

Science has also jumped into the mystery of dreams. Neuroscience has concluded dreams are a fact and after extensive research, neuroscientists have said dreams are related to REM, also known as rapid eye movement. Scientists have walked all over as to why, how, or when we dream. In conclusion, dreams are a reality, but contents of dreams are individual. Scientists have quoted different philosophical, religious, and mythological ideas to go over what the content of the dream is as each person describes after his or her sleep is over.

Some scientists have said we only dream for two hours a night and some have said it lasts anywhere from ten minutes to two hours. Scientists have also analyzed people have interconnecting dreams and why or how is a question and a mystery that I believe shall remain forever. Evidence regarding science and dreams are readily available all over the internet as search engines give us detailed descriptions and numerous research papers written by many scientists on this subject. Scientific research in union with mystics, and religious scholars show that dreams are a fact of the human existence.

As science supports the theory of dreams, scientists have also walked upon the interconnecting paths of dreams and reincarnation. Some scientists have various evidence supporting the existence of reincarnation through dreams, near death experiments, and from children who have had proof about their previous lives. Edgar Cayce, Carl Jung, Pim van Lommel, and Ian Stevenson are amongst some of the names who are well-known for their extensive research and experiments on these topics. I have given some proofs of dreams through mythological, religious, and scientific perspectives as guidance, but will leave the rest to your own choice and individual perspective, as I believe in my quotation, "Perception is but the perspective of the personal mind."

I have walked through my dreams and realized not only are dreams the complete truth of the unknown, but somehow these proofs have also synchronized dreams, resurrection, and reincarnation all blended within each faith. Dreams have led us to reincarnation and as we walk through history, we find all the proofs of reincarnation from the mythological religions walking through the Abrahamic religions as well.

Hinduism goes over reincarnation in detail. The soul is described in the Bhagavad Gita, verse 2.20, as having, "neither birth nor death at any time. He has not come into being, does not come into being, and will not come into being. He is unborn, eternal, ever-existing and primeval. He is not slain when the body is slain" (Prabhupāda 86). The text goes further in verse 2.22 in explaining "As a person puts on new garments, giving up old ones, the soul similarly accepts new material bodies, giving up the old and useless ones" (Prabhupāda 89).

I believe dreams are also a part of reincarnation as well as resurrection. The soul leaves the body and reenters the body as the dream breaks, so it is then known as resurrection. I have walked to science for more help as I wanted to know if science has any evidence of reincarnation.

Science has now gone into the aspect of reincarnation as so many people have encountered this fact within their lives. I only touch upon this aspect as the evidence has come to life through the blessed doors of dreams.

Answers to so many questions but live within various religious and scientific evidence all within one click of the internet now available to all wondering minds. If an individual accepts a source or not is an individual's perception or one's own choice of path. Reincarnation and dreams have a sacred binding. They have been examined by mystics, scientists, and philosophers alike. I believe all the answers to reincarnation, rebirth, spirituality, religious, and scientific facts woven in one is called the blessed dreams.

Again, the answer differs from person to person, but the only spiritual path known to us was given through dreams. All religious groups claim they will go to Heaven. No one has traveled and come back to testify but they have faith, complete faith, and have been guided again by dreams.

What lays in my future? What happens to the past? Where are all the people who were so lively and living amongst us? The day after their death, what happens? Why do we feel like they are still around? Why do they appear in our dreams? Why have so many people witnessed ghosts or spiritual beings? Time leaves us with messages from the past, but how does the past help the present and the future? How can we the present help the past if time has but already left us by? We can foretell and forewarn the future, but what of the past? What happens?

These questions have found answers within my dream diaries. As I walk through the pages of my dreams, I have found some answers through my blessed dreams. I have awakened spiritually as I believe all the questions we but have must have an answer. Our soul carries all the answers and has the answers buried within our lost memories, lost throughout time.

If we could travel time, our answers would all be awaiting our arrival. There is a way to these answers and I believe it is through the blessed dreams. May my dreams help you to be guided throughout the questions of your life as I believe dreams are there to guide us throughout eternity. With complete faith, we walk upon this journey of life. With complete faith, we leave this Earth after our life journey but ends. In between, we are responsible to do our share for the present as the future knocks upon our door within our blessed time.

Walk with me and gain the knowledge of the unknown always waiting to guide us throughout time. Dreams are the virtues of the unknown, unseen world. Life is a Ferris wheel where we must move on. There is always another passenger on the same seat we were just occupying. Leave a message for that person as you leave the seat. May the occupants of each seat know that they must leave the seat as their time is over. The only thing we can keep with us forever is the book of our own life. We take the book within our soul and forever walk with it.

I believe, however, throughout this journey we do not get to meet the next passenger on this Ferris wheel, but we can guide the next passenger through dreams. From the ocean of the unknown, we can be their guide. I had this in my mind as I started to write my dream diaries. I have had miracles from the unknown, unseen world where all things are alive and forever on the move as time is eternal only there, the eternal and blessed dreamland. It is where reincarnation takes birth, where miracles are walking all around, where the past and future are but the perception of the beholder, where the dead and living walk side by side as time is but frozen.

Throughout this collection of dreams, you will know how even throughout time and tide, all but is found throughout the dreamland. Come and walk with me as we discover the magical wonders of my dream diaries.

Throughout this journey, I ask you to have as a companion, faith for I believe where there is no hope, there is but one. I call her faith. Even when all is but lost, it is even then like an ark, our faith stays behind holding us afloat within this journey of life.

Today, we have scientific research examining yes, without a reasonable doubt, dreams and reincarnation do exist. We depend on science to prove wrong and right. Science has changed its views so many times about why and how we see dreams even though scientists have said yes dreams do exist. They are still trying to figure out why, how, and when we dream. They remain very elusive about this subject, as even after all this time, there is no evidence of why. Fascinated they are as even to this day, no one can say why we have dreams, or the facts behind reincarnation. To this day, so many people have witnessed this firsthand with the doctors to testify.

Miracles are just that, miracles. From the Jewish texts to the Christian Bible, to the Muslim Quran to the Egyptian mythology to the Hindu texts, even to this day, all different faiths have based the spiritual aspects of a religion on dreams, miracles, and messages from the beyond.

Travel through my dream diaries as you shall see the dead passing on messages to the future, coming and forewarning us as we travel to the future. Messages also come from the past to the future, all through dreams.

I believe there is only one truth and that is the complete truth. There is the unknown, unseen world we are but not aware of and this is but called the miracle of life.

I want all of you to walk with me as I retell my dreams through my dream diaries. My dreams are my own perspective, my own source. The best part of any dream is there is a firsthand witness and I am the only witness, firsthand. These are my words as I have seen them. With complete honor as my witness and faith as my guide, my dreams have become alive through the pages of my dream diaries.

There are a lot of dream decoding dictionaries available all over this globe, proving dreams are but a part of our existence. May my dreams be a positive guide in your life. May they help you within your faith and belief. May they guide you back to your house of beliefs as you take hand in hand all your neighbors and build a neighborhood of humans with the basic moral values under your roofs called humanity.

Edgar Cayce had said, "Each one who has a soul has a psychic power—but remember, brother, there are no shortcuts to God!" (Edgar Cayce reading 5392-1).[2]

I believe in psychic powers and that the power of good always prevails throughout eternity. I believe amongst all the questions, there is an answer within each soul as we carry the

---

[2] Edgar Cayce Readings © 1971, 1993-2007 by the Edgar Cayce Foundation. All Rights Reserved.

complete answer. It is as we have awakened from our sleep, we have made our entry onto Earth.

Just like every morning after a long night's sleep, we wake up and know we had a dream, but can't quite remember what it was about, may we the humans individually awaken from this deep sleep, and become like the saints, the priests, the religious scholars, the monks, the teachers, and the psychics of the world. I believe every single one of us carries this ability amongst our lost qualities.

With this belief, I have kept a journal, a dream journal for all the creation of The Creator. My only goal is may you find the peace and solace your soul but seeks through these dreams.

Dreams are the unknown sacred lighthouse guiding all throughout eternity. As our Earthly vehicle rests for the day, our soul awakens and travels through the unknown, unseen path always trying to guide us within our awakening life. Dreams are the mystical journey through the land of the unknown, where time is eternal and all the blessings of the eternal peace are found.

Throughout history, scholars, saints, and psychics have tried to decode the mystery of the dreams of many, yet we remain in this land of mystery. In this book, I have not tried to decode the mystery or the scientific evidence, religious, and philosophical aspects of this mystery. I know faith and personal belief is but the perspective of the perceiver. Everyone has his or her own right to his or her personal belief. I have written in my own words, my journey through these mysteries I have traveled and lived through. I have had blessed dreams throughout my life and I believe it is time I must write about my miracles of life.

All the time, I have upon my hands, the blessings of The Omnipotent as I travel this life with honor, blessings, and always humanity. All my books have the theme of inspiration, devotion, meditation, and spirituality as these are the core of my belief.

Throughout time, we the humans have had guidance from the unknown guiding us throughout this journey of life. At all times, I have kept a personal dream diary for my personal guidance. May these dreams guide and help all toward the spiritual unknown that we all know guides us throughout eternity. I know I am but the creation as The Creator guides and sends us these holy dreams and always strangers as guiding Angels.

From the past to the present, through the future, we were, are, and always shall be guided by The Creator through the spiritual world we all but know and always looked for, called miracles. In this book, I have listed the miracles of my life as they have landed upon my door. I call this book, *Spiritual Lighthouse: The Dream Diaries of Ann Marie Ruby.*

CHAPTER ONE

Messages From The Grave, All Thirteen Are Back

"Death is but the separation of a vehicle and soul, for as the soul travels time, she becomes eternal through the mystical eternity."

-Ann Marie Ruby

August 1, 2011

Potomac, Maryland, a very special place where I had been most of my life. The Potomac River, and the Great Falls Park are where I had spent days just watching the waterfall and water. The Swains Lock C&O Canal was a peaceful piece of haven.

Life was very busy as the greater Washington, D.C. metropolitan area had no time for any break and life. For me at least, it seemed like a marathon where everyone was competing to stay ahead of each other. For my soul, this was a very difficult period of my life. I forgot to live and just became a vehicle that kept on going without a break. I had blessings within my life where curses also appeared as a curse is but the consort of a blessing.

On a very dark and cloudy night, as the storm was brewing outside with lightning and thunder roaring her anger throughout the lands, I had a very awakening dream. It was very late in the night as I was looking outside through my window. The night skies looked so beautiful as Mother Nature was displaying a concert over the Potomac River, where she had wind as her dancer, lightning as her light, and thunder as her sound crew. All along, she had rain as her singer, singing for all of whom were still up and watching her like I was.

Her participating artists were lightning, thunder, rain, wind, and for extra lights, she had the stars twinkling all over the dark skyline. My sleep had overtaken my tired body as the following dream had come for a visit.

2

I was so confused as to where I was. All the houses looked like old European colonial homes. I was walking on a hillside and had entered a huge white mansion with a portico and a circular driveway. The house had ocean views with guest quarters, a tennis court, and a huge indoor swimming pool.

I somehow felt uncomfortable walking into this house. Within my soul, I knew all the luxuries of life can't change me in any way. There were dim lights all around the house and for some reason, I had reservations about entering the house. Then, I saw Archangel Gabriel had stood next to me. I asked him, "Where am I? Why do I feel so scared as if I am standing within the house of evil?"

He held my hands and told me, "Watch what is in front of you." I saw within a room, there laid a body in a coffin. The coffin was open as I saw within the box, laid a very elegantly dressed man. There were people all around the body as they were reciting a voodoo prayer or something. I then heard a woman and a man talking to themselves as they said, "For thousands of years, we have taken care of him and finally he is waking up." The man said, "All shall be fine after he awakens."

I saw then the crowd was chanting, as they said they had shared these responsibilities from the time of Christ, through the current days. Every forty-five years or so, the caretakers changed yet they have kept this secret from years ago. Then, I saw within another room of the same house, the same woman and man had tried to feed people something black. They had a black ball type fruit and glasses full of a black juice they had offered to all of the guests. As

3

people had taken this contaminated food, they became a sinner and had no control over themselves.

I watched all different men and women entering with complete faith, yet they had no control over themselves as they had left. I saw there were a few teenagers who had resisted the fruit and drinks. One girl had told her siblings something just feels wrong and that she will resist the temptations as she knew these would go directly against the Commandments. I knew she was a Jew, and she walked out of the room.

Then, I saw there was another girl who started to cry as she kept on repeating this is a sin and it feels so wrong. She ran out asking The Holy Spirit to guide her. I then watched an Indian girl kept on reciting, "Jai Sri Krishna," as she walked out with her friends. I knew this evil group of people live within our communities, yet they somehow have hidden bodies in their basement under a huge building somewhere, and kept these bodies stored somehow throughout the years.

They beautify the bodies every few years and keep the dead alive within these coffin boxes. I knew the bodies were dead, yet they were alive and I felt creepy as I knew the "coffin box man" (as I call him) was watching everything happening all around him. Even in death, it was as if he still ruled. I heard him whisper from the coffin that he would devour all the children of God. He said he will awaken within forty-five days, years, months, or something, I couldn't remember.

I watched Archangel Gabriel as he said, "The Lord had said dust to dust, ashes to ashes, yet these people have stored these bodies thinking they will rise again." As we left, I heard the people repeat, "He shall rise again, and this time blood shall be spilled, for we shall take all the people astray." I knew he was the beast as I walked out of the house.

I then held on to the hands of Archangel Gabriel as I shivered through to my bones. The sun was shining above the sky. It was warm and cozy, yet I shivered and trembled in fear. The Holy Archangel had said, "Let us go for a walk." I had walked out with him as I was so frightened after this dream. I told him, "I don't even watch horror movies. I really am a soft person and that was a lot for me." He hugged me as then I saw Archangel Michael was also standing with us as he said, "Then, now let us walk to another place."

I saw we were walking in a European country, on a cliff, near a river. I saw we were walking on a curvy road. The river was on our right and there was a bazaar on our left. This was all on a hillside and I could hear the river running below. I knew without even watching, there were rocks under the hill as the water left displaying a calming sense of relief within my soul. I watched white doves fly over us and I knew The Holy Spirit was watching over us from everywhere. I watched the sky over the river had a beautiful rainbow smiling at us as she reminded me, all shall be all right as we just have a hurdle ahead of us.

The Holy Archangels smiled at me as they could read my mind and reassured me everything shall be alright. I knew there were more bridges to cross. I wondered, what do I have in store for me now?

I then saw an elderly man running across the bridge over the river. I thought there was a ferry boat crossing people between two countries. I heard the elderly man was crying as he screamed and shouted, "All the boys were crucified like thieves! All of them were killed one by one. How had they killed him and what do they think? That they can get away with murder?" He was shouting at everyone, yet I did not fear him. Rather, I felt this strange pull towards him as if I could feel his pain.

The man was running as he cried out to the open skies, "They killed all thirteen of them. All thirteen will be back! The Lord shall bring all of them back! As The Lord promised, the dead shall rise." I saw the man crying and screaming about this all the way to a bazaar.

There within the bazaar, I saw the same man and the same woman from my earlier part of the dream walking. I could feel the same chill within my bones as I saw within her hands, she still had some black ball looking things and she was placing them with the foods that people were about to purchase. I wanted to shout and prevent all from buying anything, yet I could only watch as this was a dream. The couple was dressed differently like they had gone back in time.

I saw her laugh like a crazy woman as she watched the elderly man. She walked past him and told him, "You could do nothing to save them." The man who accompanied her just followed her and said nothing. I wondered, how did this man follow an evil woman unless he too was evil? The woman screamed and shouted as she bragged, "Christ could do nothing and neither could he save anyone of you."

The elderly man cried and watched all of this as he had no one speaking for him. The bazaar was full of people and all the people just watched and said nothing. As I watched this, I asked The Holy Archangels, "What is going on?" They watched me and said, "The End of Time is but upon us and all realize within all religious groups that this prediction has been given. The Angels shall walk upon this world, but do remember, so shall the beast and his group." I asked them, "What is going on? How is evil so strong?" They answered, "But The Lord knows all things."

I watched the elderly man come closer to us as he watched The Holy Archangels, straight in the eyes and asked them, "The Lord shall be back, right? And so, shall all thirteen. They shall all be back." The Archangels repeated, "Time is but an illusion and know for The Lord all is but present. They are back." The man jumped in joy and cried out to the skies, "They are back! All thirteen are back!"

I asked The Archangels, "The crown of the Virgin Mary has twelve stars?" I then thought out loud as I watched The Holy Angels only watch me, "The Lord shall also be back as all The Angels and the saints shall walk upon this Earth again."

I woke up from a very scary dream. I cried for the elderly man who was crying at the loss of his son. I realized his son must have been a companion of Jesus Christ. I cried for the incident from years ago, as if it just had happened. I cried for all the people whom were left behind after the crucifixion. I never had thought what all the family members had gone through. I knew all shall be okay as time is but an illusion for all humans.

I did not fear the beast at all as I knew, no beast nor evil shall touch me, for I have the glad tidings of my Lord. I know this world, within her chest, has evil and good. We must always choose good over bad and the choice is easy with basic moral values. Temptation is attractive, yet it smells foul if only you keep your sixth sense alive within your basic senses.

After the coffin man dream, I knew yes, even within this time period, people do believe in evil. I don't know if people still worship the dead and keep the dead alive, but I know there is a beast and all we must do is keep the basic moral values alive within our soul. I have a very soft spot for the elderly gentleman as I had watched his pain as he had buried his son. I knew he had complete faith within The Lord and could see the future as he had seen The Lord brought back all The Lord's sacred souls as The Lord willed.

I loved the complete faith of this man in his Lord. I knew he was lucky as even without his knowledge, The Angels were watching over him always. According to the Bible, the dead shall rise. "For the Lord himself shall descend from heaven with a shout, with the voice of the archangel, and with the trump of God: and the dead in Christ shall rise first" (*King James Version*, 1 Thessalonians 4: 16-17)

Also according to the Bible, The Angels shall rule the Earth at the End of Time as it says,

"And then shall appear the sign of the Son of man in heaven: and then shall all the tribes of the earth mourn, and they shall see the Son of man coming in the clouds of heaven with power and great glory. And he shall send his angels with a great sound of a trumpet, and they shall gather together his elect from the four winds, from one end of heaven to the other" (*King James Version*, Matthew 24: 30-31)

These dreams are beyond my explanation, yet I find some of them within the Bible and other holy books given to mankind. For my personal belief, I only believe in good and always know eternally, good shall prevail over all that is bad. Fear is an obstacle for the soul, so I have asked fear to leave me alone as I have invited courage and blessings to my house. As I woke up and had seen the sun rising through the night's sky, I knew it was all going to be alright.

For all of you, know there is nothing to fear. Always watching over us are The Holy Archangels of Heaven for our

Creator has never left us. Forever eternally, The Lord guides us and watches over us. As always there watching, guiding, and protecting all of us from the dark ocean is The Spiritual Lighthouse.

CHAPTER TWO

Love and Kisses From A Friend

"Love travels beyond time. As she spreads her wings and flies, she but catches all throughout eternity."

-Ann Marie Ruby

August 3, 1994

Rockville, Maryland, located in Montgomery County, Maryland, better known as the greater Washington, D.C. metropolitan area. Life has its own plans as she had made me travel all around the globe, for unforeseen reasons beyond my control. I love traveling though and believe I am a much better person for that. I have lived within so many different communities, amongst all race, color, and religion. I lived in Maryland for most of my life. I felt like I would never leave this land as I loved everything about this land. Mother Nature would dress up this beautiful land from the cherry blossoms to the fall color changes.

I had just leased a very nice house and was exhausted after a long and hard move. I have moved so many times that my friends call it my way of life. I must be so used to it by now. Secret out, moving is never easy.

It was a hot summer's night, as daylight goes on forever. I love to walk outside during summer nights. I was so tired from the move that I decided to turn in early for the night.

A ring sounding like a doorbell got me unsettled as to who was here at this hour. I thought to myself, it must be another neighbor who wanted to introduce his or herself. I had neighbors pop in all throughout the day with cookies. It was an amazing feeling as I did not expect this warm welcome in these days.

I tried to get up and strangely, the sound came again from my phone. I thought I answered the phone, yet I was still in bed trying to get up. I heard a very deep voice say, "Hello sweetheart."

I recognized the voice immediately as I jumped up and welcomed my very close friend from New Orleans, Louisiana. I was standing outside with him on a hot summer night. I had no clue as to how or when I had come outside. I thought I was so sleepy, I must have awakened slowly. In front of me was a French American, elegant and elderly gentleman whom I loved like a father.

Before I could say anything, he gave me a bear hug and said in his deep voice, "How are you sweetheart? I have missed you so much."

I asked him how he found my address and why he did not call me and warn me. I had so much to show him and so much to tell him about my life. He laughed and said, "You are just as I remember. You have not changed a bit, and sweetheart before anything, I must tell you, I only have a very short amount of time. I really wanted to see you before I leave."

I asked him how long does he have and when does he have to go. He hugged me and said he did not want to waste time talking about how long he could stay, but he wants to spend quality time with me.

We went to various places all around the greater Washington, D.C. metropolitan area as we went on a short helicopter ride. The whole town looked so nice from the sky. I loved this time with my dear friend. I asked him about his wife and saw there were teardrops in his eyes as they had started to fall with the mention of her name.

He said she was busy as their eldest daughter had just found out she has cancer and was under treatment. I asked him, "What is her prognosis?" He laughed and said in his own way, "It is not her time yet. She will beat this with all of our prayers."

I told him I will pray for her and all his family as they deserve so much more than life has given them. He smiled as he spoke again, "One thing I have always believed, The Lord never gives more than what one can handle."

He kept on speaking, "Always know The Lord is watching over all of us at all times, throughout our time on Earth and beyond." I had the shivers again after so many years. I felt like, okay what is going on? Strangely, I don't remember getting dressed, or coming out on this flying adventure in the middle of the night with a dear friend who had flown all the way to Maryland from New Orleans, Louisiana. To top it up, how did he get my address as I have not shared my address with anyone yet? I was not sure I knew my address properly yet.

He was watching me and smiled as if he could read my mind. I saw we were back home and I was standing in my living room as he was watching me.

He said first, "I know you are shocked as to how I am here. I passed away a few hours ago, in New Orleans, Louisiana. As a Catholic, I lived my life to the fullest and now I am in peace. I have left behind my wife and family. They are all devastated by this death as they are all going through a hard time trying to battle with my daughter's cancer treatments. As for why I am here, I don't really know, but I was asked if I knew someone who could help me and whom I wanted to visit. I then found myself in your presence."

He then told me, "I love you like my own child and I guess I was really sad not to have seen you before I passed away, but I am glad I could see you." I had so many questions for him as to what happens after death? Why do I have these visits from the dead? But again, I saw dawn was breaking open through the night's sky. My dear friend had said his goodbyes as my sleep had broken.

I woke up to a wet pillow and my waterworks continued for a long time until I picked up the phone to make a very sacred call. The phone was answered by his wife and her voice was so strong, sweet, and loving as she was comforting me throughout our phone conversation.

She had said, "This is real family, not what we are born into, but the family we choose to have on Earth. You are our true child as therefore, you know he just passed away last night."

She also told me he had taken my name as he had taken his last breath. He died in peace as he had lived his whole life in peace, with dignity, and with courage. I did share my dream with her as she told me this is a pure miracle.

I must say this blessed couple had a blessed journey together as they had shared sweet and sour memories that keep her going. Love never dies. Even death can never separate true love, for love continues throughout time. Faces change and another couple is born as time flies by, but love continues throughout time.

I share this dream with all of you, always giving the whole truth, but keeping the identities of my friends a secret to give all involved privacy. The message I had taken from this dream is about families. It is not the families we were born into, but the families our soul but creates as she travels through life.

Have faith in this miracle word, love. Love is a relationship between a mother and her child, a father and his child, or just friends. Love is out there all over this universe. When two people fall in love, it is then I believe blessings from Heaven pour down on Earth. True love is eternal. Faces change as our Earthly vehicles change, but are always replaced with two new faces. If love is alive, the blessings from the Heavens shall be pouring on this Mother Earth of ours.

Always have faith, oh the blessed creation of The Creator. Even if you are an orphan, you too have a family on Earth if there are kind-hearted people like this couple around us. Again, from the ocean of the unknown, my friend had sent me the message of friendship, family, and miracles. One more thing, his daughter had beaten cancer as she still is living a healthy life.

Always believe in miracles guiding us from the unknown ocean, the Spiritual Lighthouse.

CHAPTER THREE

Soul To Soul: Inscribed In The House Of Heaven

"From soul to soul, mind to mind, body to body, soulmates hold on to each other, bridging a bond beyond eternity."

-Ann Marie Ruby

October 28, 2015

Seattle, Washington, my favorite city in this universe. Life has given me a chance in this city where people love, respect, and honor each other as we walk by the historical Farmers' Market, go on a daytrip to the islands in the Puget Sound, or just walk through Downtown Seattle. Life is forever moving. People are as busy as can be, going and doing their own things.

The difference is you exist. People here don't pretend to not see you, or make you feel invisible. Here, we stop and talk to each other. Even a simple smile brings the sunshine back into the foggy Seattle rain. Warm-hearted smiles of acknowledgement keep Seattle warm throughout the year. I always try to take a break from life and enjoy nature in its true glory. The Seattle rain is a beautiful concert The Creator bestows upon us. I have been in Seattle for a few years now, as more blessed dreams came upon my door.

The temperature was 50 degrees Fahrenheit. It was raining outside, and it felt like Mother Nature was giving us yet another beautiful concert. I turned into bed early and ended up in another mysterious land of The Creator.

In front of me, there was a beautiful cottage with a front porch that was beautifully decorated. There were white rocking chairs with blue cushions, and huge wicker baskets hanging as they were filled with colorful flowers. I stood there and smelled the flowers for a long time until I saw the front door was ajar and all the windows were open. Ceiling fans were making their presence known as they were dancing with the white sheer curtains blowing in the air.

The house looked like a very old stone cottage with all the touches of modern amenities blanketed by the olden charm. There was a huge grandfather clock singing his tune in the corner. The kitchen looked like it was very well used. There was a smell of fresh baked bread. A fruit basket filled with fresh fruits and vegetables was lying around the kitchen.

The living room had all blue and white furniture and the same theme went all over the house. I saw the evidence of love, laughter, and life all around the house. Strange, I felt right at home as if I just entered the pure bliss of Heaven. It was a small, charming cottage right out of a painter's canvas, yet I could feel, smell, and hold on to the warmth and serenity that was within this house.

I just wanted to be there and never leave the house. The strangest thing was that I did not even know where I was or who owned the house, how I had appeared there, but just had this feeling of serenity and peace all over my soul.

I walked from one room to another room as I heard the sounds coming from one of the rooms. I walked into a room where men were in meditation. I never felt like a stranger walking in a stranger's home and this feeling shocked me even more. In this room, I saw men deep in meditation as all the open windows brought a beautiful and serene breeze throughout the house.

I just wanted to see their meditation. I never wanted to leave this house as I read on top of this room, a sign that glowed in the air. The sign read, "The Holy Archangels."

I froze in spot as I knew why the house felt so peaceful. I must say I had such a big relief within my soul that I wanted to cry and shout, "Yes! I made it to Heaven!" I was enjoying my new-found peace of making it to Heaven as I saw a young man, who was wearing all white, just showered, so clean, and pure looking. He came toward me as he said, "Hi! I am Michael, Archangel Michael."

I was speechless for a while as I had told him, "Why am I here? I am just, Ann Marie Ruby." He laughed and gave me a hug. He said, "Yes, I know." We had talked for a while. I wish I had remembered, but I don't know what I talked with him about. I knew I had felt right at home and this was family.

Then, I walked into another room where it said, "The Holy Archangel Gabriel." As I saw him, he also smiled and walked with me through the house as I had talked with him for a long time. The house had in big capital letters written all over, "THE HOUSE OF THE ARCHANGELS."

I asked everyone why I was there. How had I been so lucky to be in this holy house? I knew there must be a message in here for me somehow and somewhere.

I was told by The Archangels not to give up and always know, "Where there is no hope, there is but one," as The Omnipotent always watches over. I wanted to ask what have I given up on? Life is hard. At all times, I am fighting the criticism of humans more on top of all other obstacles life brings upon our plates. One thing I always carry within my soul is faith.

I walked into another room. This room I know I have been to so many times. I felt like I knew every part of this room. Somehow, my whole life was in front of me. I saw my clothes were laid in the closet neatly with another person's clothing. I saw my pictures were hanging on the wall with another man in the same frame.

I saw The Archangels were watching over me as I had walked into the room. There was a huge wall with murals and art work all over it. The murals were also my pictures, hand drawn by a talented artist who had turned my picture into a beautiful art. The wall had my name written on it, all in capital letters. Next to my name in capital letters, it said, "SOULMATE FOREVER AND EVER." There was another name next to my name and I watched the two names come close to each other.

The wall had magical letters appear as it read, "Forever and ever, soul to soul, mind to mind, body to body, we are but one." The two names were in a heart shape and it read, "Soul to soul, forever yours." I do remember the name, but for personal reasons, I will not disclose his name. I did not know any one personally by that name and wondered why my Lord was showing me this.

As I wondered why I was being shown this dream, The Archangels replied, "Please do not give up on hope for hope blooms around the corner. As all is but lost, he is still out there, and he remains pure as you are." They told me life is complicated and when all seem lost and we find no reason to go on, we must remember The Lord has a reason for each soul. I told them I have given my soul to my Lord. They told me they knew, yet there is a human walking this Earth to whom I belong as he belongs to me too. I told them I don't believe in belonging, but just being.

They replied when he shows up, I will understand what they mean. They repeated, "You two shall be one and you will realize as he too will realize you two belong to each other." They asked me not to forget his name. I thought how could I forget his name as it is inscribed within my soul. I worried though that I will never approach any man in my life as I live a very sacred life. I am not sin free and never claim to be, but I have always tried to avoid sins if I could. I cried as I saw then in the same room, he appeared in front of me as he too touched the wall and read my name.

He asked me, "Are we dreaming again or is this reality?" I did not know the answer, but I ran toward him as I hugged him and cried for a long time. I asked him, "How do I find you? Where do I find you?" We held on to each other as I do not remember the replies to my questions.

The whole night, I prayed with The Archangels as my soulmate and I prayed all night for guidance. I woke up with his name on my lips, and I also knew I would not disclose his name to another soul. I had been praying the whole night and had awakened with a prayer within my lips. I wrote the prayers we were reciting. Strange thing was yes, I do remember some of the prayers as if they just came to me.

I have written my prayer book as a direct inspiration of The Holy Archangels.

I did not find my soulmate yet as this journal is being written. Like the messages from The Holy Archangels within the dream, I will not give up on the hope that we will meet one day. Until we do meet, I remain celibate from all sins as throughout my life, I believe we all should remain celibate and should not jump into any sinful act just because it feels and seems so lucrative. Is it hard to remain celibate? No, it is not. It is peaceful for I love my Lord and I live my life following the commandments of my Lord.

Life is a blessing when and where there are no lies or known sins. Unknown sins I try to avoid. I have written prayers of repentance for all creation of The Creator. I believe truly from my soul with pure repentance and redemption, all souls can awaken spiritually to be better human beings. The best picture I can draw for you is when you see yourself in the mirror of life and if you can forgive yourself, it is then you know, The Lord is but watching over you and everything shall be alright.

Have faith and with faith, all is achieved. I know I shall find my soulmate as from my soul I shall call upon his soul until this life but ends. Never shall I lose faith for within faith, my Lord but is. I read in the Abrahamic scriptures of the Babylonian Talmud as I was doing research for my dream diaries, Rabbi Levi said, "A man should always wait up to twenty-two years for [the fulfilment of] a good dream" ("Berakhot" 55b).

Does this mean I must wait that long? Only The Lord knows, but I believe this means each dream has certain parts that but come true within days and some parts take longer. After all, it is only time.

With complete faith, my mind, body, and soul know from the unknown ocean, always guiding us throughout eternity is my Lord's Spiritual Lighthouse.

CHAPTER FOUR

Alex: Guiding From The Beyond

"Like a night owl watching over all creation are the good spirits of eternity."

-Ann Marie Ruby

March 4, 2015

Downtown Seattle, life goes on even beyond the nights. The stars are the street lights, and there are cars moving and people walking even as dawn breaks open.

I lived one block away from the Space Needle and had a nice view of the Space Needle. A café was the first floor of the apartment complex, and a French bakery was across the building. My puppy loved to walk at nights as he loves watching other dogs go for their break time at the same time.

He loves to wag his tail as he meets his friends in the lobby. This was a night just like all the other nights and we came back home after a nice walk. I went to bed and as I fell asleep, this would turn out to be a very strange night.

I was standing in a room and I thought my apartment manager's son who was about eight months old and a very cute baby boy, had come over as his mother had no babysitter and asked for a favor. I was walking with him in my arms as he said what I thought was his first word, "Alex." He repeated this word as now he was upset at Alex and had a bad feeling.

I cuddled him and told him not to cry. Everything will be okay for life only gives us everything we can handle. I know I was talking to myself for this was a baby, but he understood and smiled as he hugged me and rested for the day.

Next, I saw I was standing in the foyer of a house where there was a loft in front of me and a huge glass room on my right-hand side. Toward my left-hand side, there was an orange tree.

I saw now on my lap, there was another boy, a baby boy who had called me Mama. I started to cry as I did not know what just happened. When had I moved out of the apartment? Am I now in my own house or somewhere else? I knew the baby's name was JR and his first name was the same as my soulmate's name from my other dreams. I was shocked as I felt old and knew this is a miracle I never expected, but how was this possible?

I saw on the right-hand side, the glass room had a baby, but his mother and his father were in the dark. I cried and told them, "No, I will help." I turned their lights on. I saw there was a family and the woman was called Sara, the father was Abraham, and they had their son. I wondered what a nice family as my son said, "Mama, Papa, and me. Family."

Then, I saw toward my left, there was a huge orange tree with fruits hanging from it. I wondered how will I go up the staircase and to the glass room or the loft upstairs for this huge orange tree was just sitting here. What does it represent? My son then picked up a leaf from the tree and said, "For me." Then, I saw a leaf from the orange tree landed upon my hand.

My son said, "Love Alex." I wondered who was this Alex my baby loves. I did not remember in my dream the first Alex dream in which the other boy was frightened by the other Alex. Yet now my baby boy kept on saying Alex and each time he said Alex, he said, "Love you Alex" and blew a kiss toward the orange tree.

I was shocked. As soon as that happened, I saw I was in the loft with huge boxes. Now, I thought we just moved into a new house and I saw my baby boy spoke his first word as he said, "Alex." I wondered why Alex? Who is Alex? I saw my husband walk into the room and said, "What? He said what? Not Mama Papa, but Alex?" I saw I was there moving into a new house with my family.

I don't remember how and when we had moved into the house, or who Alex was, but I guess life will give me the answers as time but passes by. The next morning as I went to get my mail, Sara, my apartment manager, stopped me and asked if I could do her a favor. I was so shocked for I knew my dreams come true but some of them have taken four years to one year or less, but what was going on?

I told Sara about my dream and shared the name Alex. Who was Alex and why was her son so upset about Alex? I thought in my dream, the baby was frightened and did not like him. I did ask Sara to keep Alex in her mind. I did babysit her son that day as a friend and how could I not when the reward was such a cute baby. It was my blessing to watch over a baby.

Within a few days, Sara and I both were astounded when someone named Alex had moved into the apartment right below my apartment. After a few days of moving in, he went through a bad divorce as the fight between the couple had awakened all in the apartment complex. Then, Alex started to bang on the walls and had kept all within the building awake throughout the night. He had become scary and Sara had asked me if I want, she will give a notice to him.

I had told Sara no, not to trouble anyone for in my life, I don't want to ever complain or become a trouble for anyone. I was thinking of buying a house and would just buy sooner than later. I knew though for me to buy a house, I must find the right house.

I moved into my own house as more dreams had come to complete this dream. After many more dreams pointed me toward the Netherlands, I had taken a blessed trip to the Netherlands. My trip had taught me all women and men in their fifties are called Sara and Abraham. I also learned the orange tree represents the Royal family and Willem-Alexander is the kind-hearted King of the Netherlands.

I smiled as I knew a boy from the future will also love this kind King. I guess I will become fifty by the time life blesses me with these gifts of eternity.

I share this dream as a message to all that within life, The Lord watches over all even when we think why is this happening to me. I love Seattle and I was living in a European style apartment complex I really liked, but maybe The Lord was showing me other things. I don't know what the future but holds in store for me as I keep on reminding myself about the Jewish scriptures as it said some dreams take years to come true as some parts become true within days, and some parts in due time.

I have complete faith in my Lord and I am blessed to have this life and this day to repent, redeem, and awaken. Each morning is but a new beginning and a new blessing. I will never forget what the blessings of today mean for the love of tomorrow for then we are but lost. Hope and faith are what keep me going for I know as we live through the blessings of today, tomorrow shall be a new beginning.

Until dawn breaks open with a new day, keep hope alive. For me forever and for you always, remember from the unknown ocean of life, we are being guided by The Creator through the Spiritual Lighthouse.

CHAPTER FIVE

A Stranger's Knock Is But A Blessing In Disguise

"Never close the doors to blessings, for she knocks when you are but not watching."

-Ann Marie Ruby

February 6, 2016

I was busy looking at houses all throughout Seattle. Washington State is a beautiful state with so much to offer. The Puget Sound, Chambers Bay, the Cascades Mountains, and the Olympic Mountains all stand out creating a picturesque view. I got to see so much more as I had toured throughout the real faces of this state looking for a place where I would find the house of my dreams.

I drove all the way from Downtown Seattle through Olympia and I really fell in love with the Tacoma area. I did not see any particular house as I needed to know where to buy the house. I prayed to The Lord up in Heaven to guide me through this chapter of my life. This night, I prayed for I needed guidance.

I did not pray for a house or anything personal, but always to be guided and that never may I go astray and end up on the wrong path. Life teaches us through examination of faith. I always pray to my Lord, blessed be whatever comes upon my plate. Blessed be, may I be able to handle it with dignity, honor, and courage.

Sleep finally took over my mind and body as my soul traveled again to this strange world. I was sitting in a room where I had a huge antique table. I was typing on my laptop. I saw in the room there was Sara. I asked her, "You are Sara and Brad is your husband?" She said, "No, his name is Bert and yes, I am Sara." I was confused as this was not Sara the apartment manager. Who was she? That is when into the room came a very elegant woman who introduced herself as Margaret.

She was watching over me as I saw in the room appeared Archangel Michael. I went and hugged him. As he kissed my head, I told him, "I know you forever, Archangel Michael." He laughed and gave me a hug as he said, "Yes and I ask you again to write the songs." I was shocked and said, "Songs? No, I have not published anything yet, but I have them on my laptop and maybe I will have them published." He laughed and said, "These are people who need prayers and you know them." I asked him, "How do I know them if I have never met them?"

Sara said, "Did you find the house yet? I know it is your house and she will find you." I watched her and thought what was she talking about. That is when I saw Margaret for the first time say she does not know where Alex is, but she has found his parents. I asked them where was Alex and they said he was somewhere else and they await his arrival.

I was in a strange house with people whom I have never met. I wondered who is this Alex everyone keeps talking about? I asked, "Why the rush for a house? I can wait a few months and take it slowly."

That is when Archangel Michael spoke, "The apartment has new tenants and drug dealers have moved in. A lot of sin and sinners are coming within this area. Remember always where there is sin, there is suffering and what humans call and say unfair and unjust from the above. Truth be told, it is but the humans who bring this and do all this to each other. We just guide and try to help all from falling prey to each other."

33

We spoke for a long time when I got to know Sara, Bert, and Margaret much better. My dream broke and that morning, I had gone to see a house within the greater Seattle area. I had seen three houses and the last one had water views with a nice cottage feeling, but I still had my doubts.

As I was walking out of the kitchen, my friend, one of the many who were with me, opened the kitchen cabinet to see the drawers. Within the drawers there was an album which was left by the original owner of the house. Within this album there were Sara, Bert, Margaret, and Alex. I had shared the dreams with all my friends before coming here.

We sat and read through the album of photos and newspaper clippings. We only saw that they were a family and Alex had passed away in a plane crash, but no one knows how. It was his private small plane. Sara and Bert were the parents of Alex, and Margaret was the daughter-in-law. They had details of their life stories left for me. The owners had passed on the album I still own and within it stands in black and white the life stories from the past.

The house in between was owned by others. I knew I had finally found my house as she was a blessed house. I must say I felt so strange as I had come home and Googled all about the original owners. I had found out they were such a peace-loving Catholic and Jewish family.

The dream stays within my heart as I feel like a blessed family member not related by blood, but through the bridge of time.

Life is a miracle and it is true even life lives on forever through miracles of life.

On that same day, as I went to my apartment, next to my apartment complex, a fight was going on in between two drug dealers. All the people just walked past the drug dealers. I wanted to say something, but as a hair salon stylist walked out, he pulled me inside. I asked him, "What is going on?" He told me, "Never get involved for otherwise you will be the innocent victim." I cried as I walked back to my apartment which never felt like home again.

How can a place be home if there is no peace? I live my life to spread peace. I remembered Archangel Michael's words, "Write." I had bought the house within a week of viewing it and moved in on February 26, 2016. I published my first book in February of 2017. As a single woman, what can I do to help anyone? I thought about this and on the same antique table Margaret had owned, passed by all the owners to me, I have written my books and yes, the prayer book I call *Spiritual Songs*, and now my dream diaries.

Message for all of you, know the truth is out there beyond the human mind and knowledge. Seek, knock, and ask for guidance and always believe in the power of The Creator. Always have faith and know the stranger that just knocked upon your door is but a blessing in disguise. For everyone, always guiding us from the vast, dark ocean is the Spiritual Lighthouse.

CHAPTER SIX

Danger Is But The Unwelcomed Guest Of Life

"Keep an eye out for danger, for she warns not of her arrival, but just walks in as an unwelcomed guest."

-Ann Marie Ruby

July 12, 2017

Life's eternal blessings are found when they are not searched for. I have a puppy who has taught me so much about life without saying even a word. He knows my feelings even more than I know myself. He knows when I am sad and tries to entertain me with his ball and wants to share all his toys. He waits for me at the window or the door, wagging his tail, as I enter the house. For him, I had become an animal lover and I know how all life on this Earth are but the beloved creation of The Creator.

Patches loves his walking time as he wags his little tail and any animal lover will know a wagging tail and jumping all around in joy brings peace within the hearts of all. Strangest thing is I forget sometimes he is not human, for he is my little boy.

This was another hot summer day in Seattle as we turned in for the night. Patches went to his room and his very comfy bed. I went to my room and watched the ferries cross over the Puget Sound. As the glorious moon was shining over all, she brought joy within the souls of all the viewers. I love all that Mother Nature but brings upon our plates, the stormy nights and the beautiful summer nights. This was a very peaceful night as I just finished my sixth book and was working on my dream diaries. Sleep had finally taken over and I had the following dream.

I was in a house where I saw a beautiful wisteria grew tall and high, flowering within her true beauty. A teenager was with me on this afternoon walk. She is a spiritual friend who even though young, is a very admirable person. I was admiring the tall trees all around my house as I saw a huge orange colored dog run toward Patches, my puppy.

My friend lifted Patches up in her arms as Patches had started running for his life. I was worried what was going on? Who is this dog and why was she in my garden running after my dog? I asked my friend and Patches just to sit and not say anything. I tried to go in between the huge dog and my friend who was carrying Patches. My friend carried my puppy and ran as she bumped into something. I thought something hit her as it was not clear. I thought she got hurt and was hit by a waste management truck. I started to run for my friend as my dream shifted a little and I saw myself on my knees praying.

I saw then Jesus Christ had walked into my house as he picked up some things from my house. He called these things obstacles and threw them out. He asked me if I had anything I would like to say. I started to cry and told him, "I have spent all my life praying, but today I want a special prayer for a very special friend who as a Christian follows all the laws of the land and above all, her religion to the core."

I told him, "We think we were born in the wrong era. Somehow, we should have been in your time." He laughed and as I hugged him, he said, "All shall be okay. Watch."

In front of me, I saw again the other dog, but Christ had changed something about the dog. Then, he took care of the dog as he brought back my friend. He kissed both our heads and said this shall all be a safe road now. He said, "The path is always the same, but with prayers and caution, you can change the dangers of life into blessings traveling upon the same path. Dreams are a guide to the future and at times to the past." I saw Jesus Christ had told me to watch. Then, I saw in the family room was standing a man who he said was my soulmate.

I kept on asking Jesus Christ for guidance in life as he was smiling and said you shall find him. My dream broke with a blessed feeling as I had seen Christ. I spent the whole day like I was in Paradise as I had seen Christ.

Two days after I had seen the dream, today is July 14th as I am writing this dream, a strange fearful event had taken place in my life. I was walking with my friend who loves my puppy and had not recalled my dream from two nights ago. I had only remembered Jesus Christ as the days had progressed. Today is trash day. A neighbor who had moved in a few months after I had, was standing on her porch. I was standing and walking slowly as I love to watch my garden grow. The beautiful summer flowers were blooming in colors, and yes, I admire my flowers every day.

My friend and Patches were playing as they were walking ahead of me. Suddenly there was a huge orange dog, that belongs to my neighbor, running toward us. My neighbor was trying to control the dog, but could not. My puppy is very small in size and jumped up within the arms of my friend. He was trying to hide instead of bark. The huge dog was then biting my puppy and tried to hurt my friend and me as I tried to stand in between them.

It was so scary how the owner could not control the dog which was too big in size. She repeated they have the dog always inside and on leash because the dog is not friendly and tries to hurt others without understanding. I would have sat down and talked with her and even would have tried to find a solution for her situation, but at that time I was only thinking to save my friend and my puppy.

Suddenly, I started to pray as I tried to get the dog to stop. My friend took that break and ran toward the trash can. The world froze in front of me as I saw right behind my trash can was my wisteria and by the wisteria, was a huge life size statue of the Virgin Mary.

I saw my friend hid behind the trash can as the owner of the dog took her dog finally within control as her family members all just watched her in a blank stare. All the time, I tried to stand in between the dog and my friend and Patches, but somehow the dog just wanted to bite my baby puppy and my friend.

I saw the Virgin Mary statue standing in my garden, in peace and harmony, within all the flowers and knew the power of a prayer is so much more than any human knowledge. Tears fell nonstop as I knew my faith had saved the life of my friend and puppy. I saw within my garden, I have kept the gifts of my Hindu, Buddhist, and Christian family friends. I felt like today, such a big miracle had just taken place.

I know this miracle would only be at the intervention of the Heavens above. The neighbors eventually apologized as they got their dog. By the way, the owner is a veterinarian who had rescued this dog and was trying to train her. I saw the trash can and realized in my dream, there was a truck with waste management written all over it and my friend had bumped into it with a very tragic ending.

But here today, the truck turned out to be a trash can with the same name written on it. Nearby was the statue of the Holy Virgin standing tall and reminding me this day, the prayers were answered. I cried for a long time as I had another surprise that day when this dear friend's sister had told me she had seen a dream two nights ago as she too writes all her dreams as all my friends do and share with me.

She had shared her dream with me as I had shared mine. Strange we both totally forgot about the dreams as life goes on. She had seen Patches was bitten by an orange dog and was limping. She also had written that she brought the puppy to my house and was praying. As Patches was healed, her dream had broken.

I have shared my dreams with very few of my close friends, who have become spiritually awakened as they too see holy dreams. Anyone thinking about what happened to the neighbor and her dog, well I have never sued anyone in my life and I do not believe there is any reason to be the one all of us hate to become. I forgive and walk forward with my life.

I, however, did tell her she needs to put a leash on her dog and always keep the dog under observation for we live in a community with children who walk with and without adult supervision, as at times parents walk slowly talking to each other and children walk ahead of them. I pray my new neighbor does keep her dog on a leash. Only the future shall guide us.

My dream came true within two days, at least one part of my dream. The part that I really don't talk about is my soulmate. As I wait for him, I have complete faith in my Lord The Omnipotent. My message for all of you is please take care of your actions. May they not cause any harm or be of danger to another soul who might be a stranger to you but a beloved devotee of The Omnipotent or a non-believer in your eyes.

For within each soul, there are peace and blessings we but carry within our journey of life. Live within the basic moral values and never be The Judge. Always know there might be danger around the corner. Always be careful and be safe as life keeps passing by us and all we have for each other are the lessons learned from the books of life.

To guide and keep all but safe, always from the unknown ocean of life, standing still guiding all of whom but seek, forever is the Spiritual Lighthouse.

CHAPTER SEVEN

Have You Written The Songs Yet?

"Peace and serenity sing through the winds of eternity through the blessed songs of prayers."

-Ann Marie Ruby

June 9, 2012

Orlando, Florida, the warm sunshine, Spanish style houses, and palm trees. Life feels like being on a vacation all the time. I loved being in Florida and had bought a Spanish style single family home thinking this is it, never moving again. But, life had other plans for me. Life for me had been one struggle after another. Throughout all the storms of life, I have never lost faith in my Lord, my Lord's ways, and my Lord's word. My prayer forever was, is, and shall always be, "May my Lord's will always prevail." With complete faith, I walk into all the storms life but brings upon my door.

I was packing again for another move, though this time by choice. I was ready to move again as life had it, Florida was not to be my home for too long. This is one of those nights when I had for company, all my tears. Some nights appear in life when everything seems cold and a shivering chill comes down within the mind, body, and soul.

You stay awake thinking is there anything I could do differently? You wonder what to do when you are but a prey of those people who live on making everyone's lives miserable with no thought. They sleep peacefully yet have no care how their actions could ruin a person's life. For all of you, I ask on this day, please think before you say anything or be the reason of pain and destruction for the other one standing next to you. I have some family members who have caused immense pain as I remained silent. Without saying anything, I had walked away.

My biggest fault is I believe in all race, color, and religion. I had fallen asleep with all the waterworks as my companions when I had the following dream.

I was in a high-rise apartment and I had come downstairs to get the mail. The elevator had jammed and we were all stuck in the elevator. I say "we" as I saw some of my friends were there with me. We waited as the elevator opened and the firefighters were all crowded in the lobby. There were a lot of firefighters who had the words "Angels of God" written on their clothes. I thought that was a nice name for the firefighters. I walked out and was glad to be safe.

Our elevator had rocked up and down and was stuck in between two floors as we walked out with the help of a nice gentleman whom I had seen repeatedly. I held on to him as he watched me. He asked me to be safe and to wait for him. He said to never give up as days will pass and even if all seem lost, we will unite.

I went to a corner of the lobby where I bumped into a firefighter who asked me, "Ann Marie, have you written the songs yet?" I asked him, "What songs? I only write prayers for my Lord." He smiled and said, "Yes, we know." I asked him, "What? How? I have never shared this with anyone. How do you know?"

He asked, "May I have a hug?" I said, "Yes, sure. Who are you?" He replied, "Archangel Michael. I am glad you are finally out of the elevator." I cried as he gave me a bear hug and said, "Life is

45

a blessing. Always know within all the struggles and sorrows of life, tomorrow shall come with the sun shining about as dawn breaks open after the dark night's sky."

I had shared all my life stories with him and asked him for guidance. He smiled and asked me again and again why have I not written the songs yet. I saw there were more people with him and he smiled as he introduced me to others. I kept thinking when had I moved into this apartment and how did this elevator get stuck? Had I died? Is that why I am here?

Archangel Michael laughed and reassured me I have not died, and that I still have a few jobs I must complete, one of which is writing the songs. He also smiled and said, "Your soulmate still awaits your union. As life goes on, you shall find him."

I woke up crying for a long time as I had this dream. In my heart, I knew life was really a struggle, so I did not know how I would be able to get my prayer book out. I had shared this dream with very few close friends. I forgot all about this dream as life had brought obstacles as companions in my life, until one day when life had given me a strange knock upon my door.

In 2014, I was living in Downtown Seattle in a high-rise apartment. I went downstairs to the lobby to get my mail. The elevator had stopped, and a few people and I were stuck in the elevator for a while until someone opened the elevator from the outside. We all walked out as we were not even panicked for this elevator always did this.

As we all walked outside, there were firefighters and the lobby was really crowded. I thought maybe I would use the staircase this time. I would have to go ten floors up, but I had done that before. After getting the mail, I thought okay, I'll go up the staircase as I saw the elevator shaft was left open.

A person had on a t-shirt and printed on the shirt was the word "Angels." He said, "Hey don't panic. It's the End of Time anyway and we are all here."

This was a very nice and polite person who was always friendly. This incident reminded me of my dream and I thought maybe my prayer book should be out now. Somehow, I had taken life as a struggle and lived for peace and serenity, never letting the struggles of life take control over me, but always trying to find peace amongst everything. Life finally became a blessing as I learned to take life as a blessing amongst all the struggles and endeavors of life.

I started to write all my dreams and my prayers in a diary for myself, always keeping them private and within my sacred chest. I again ignored this dream for a long period of time until 2017 when another dream had landed upon my door.

I was walking by a river where I heard sounds of people crying and asking for help. I knew I could do nothing but pray. I kept on hearing the words of Archangel Michael, "Have you written the songs yet?" I cried and looked upon the sky for help and said, "Please help. I don't want to be in public and don't want any attention, positive or negative, either way."

I then saw as tears rolled, I had taken all my prayers and called them the songs of life.

I placed my prayers on individual papers. Then, I placed them in individual bottles and let them float in a river. I prayed, "May they reach the people who but need them." I saw my prayers were glowing in the dark and became like candles of hope. I stood up and prayed for all as I recited, "May these songs be the lighthouse for all of whom but seek." I saw within my hands, I had a few books and I knew one book was called *Spiritual Songs*.

As I woke up this time, I knew this is it. I must do my share and help those who need a little support, or prayers to awaken each creation individually and spiritually. When they need to share a sweet song with their Creator, may they find solace through my songs as I did. After years of fighting a war within my soul, I knew I had to get out of the elevator and even if it helps one soul, let that soul find peace through my words.

I have had guidance from the Heavens above. The Holy Archangels have guided me throughout my dreams as I have written throughout my dream diaries. I kept leaving all the messages from the Heavens above behind, for my fear of this world. I finally had summoned upon the courage and published my very special Spiritual Collection.

Dear Holy Archangels of the Heavens above, I have published my songs as I had promised. I named her, *Spiritual Songs: Letters From My Chest*. I have also written my daily inspirational quotations, and I call her *Spiritual Ark: The Enchanted Journey Of*

Timeless Quotations. This book, my dream diaries, will be my seventh book. May fear not hold anyone behind for if courage could be summoned up, it would be called the love of an Angel in disguise.

For all, I would like to say never give up on anything. Even when all but seem lost or when life knocks you down, shake her hand with a smile and let her know even if life gives you no chance, you want to give her a chance. Remember even when all is lost, and you feel lost and stranded amongst the dark night's ocean, always with a twinkle in her eyes and a smile made from light, guiding all from the unknown is the Spiritual Lighthouse.

CHAPTER EIGHT

Land Chooses Her Leader To Keep Her Children Safe

"Leaders are but blessings, given to us by the Heavens above for it is they who but spread an umbrella of peace and harmony throughout the lands for eternity."

-Ann Marie Ruby

April 7, 2016

This night, I sat outside and watched the ferry boats cross the Puget Sound. I saw birds flying and wondered where do they go at sunset as they start to fly in groups. Maybe, they too enjoy the beautiful sunset and stay outside like me into the late night and just meditate with these serene sights of Mother Earth.

I thought about my ability to see the future, the past, and sometimes unexpected events of my life and the people around me. Sometimes, I also see wonders of the future as they knock upon my door. I do not, however, call myself a psychic or a healer. I have had different forms of dreams. I have seen warnings from the future as I had seen the 9/11 attack dream, yet had no idea what it was until it was in front of me on the screen of my television and within the painful tears of my friends and family.

I had seen Chelsea Clinton in tears with her father as they told me Hillary Clinton had lost the election. I had seen Donald Trump praying to The Lord for guidance. I have kept all these dreams out of my dream diaries as I could only choose a few of my dreams. I have, however, picked this dream as it was a total shock to me for as an American, I know my President and I am proud to say I do know my State Governor, but I have no clue about any world leaders or other countries that also have their own problems and gifts of life.

So naïve, I call myself, as I had not paid any mind to the world we live in, but was only worried about my small world around me. My dreams, however, were not naïve or ignorant and therefore I know and believe I am blessed through the blessed dreams. It is true, I see my own life and the lives of people around me in my blessed dreams. Yet, I also see strangers, strange lands, and places where I had never laid my feet or eyes upon and never could I dream about them without the blessings of my Lord and my Lord's will. I believe it is always my Lord's will that I see these miracles.

Dreams haunted me as they landed upon my door. Dreams about a faraway land kept coming to me over the years. I would walk past windmills upon a flat land who herself had called me within my dreams. There was a fisherman's village where I kept finding myself. I saw fishing boats and I knew I have been there, but I could not figure out how. I knew there was a flood somewhere and everything was flooded. I knew it could have been worse, but somehow my prayers were with this land.

These dreams have been with me for years as I would awaken each morning trying to figure out where I was. Why had I seen a castle which had a moat and a bridge? Never in my life had I heard of these places nor had I wanted to consider them out of fear. I don't know what I feared. I knew these dreams were related to the topic of reincarnation which I had avoided at any cost.

I will talk about these dreams in the next few chapters as I like to only write about one dream at a time. All these dreams stayed with me for years until one night a strange dream haunted me again. This time, a person knocked upon my door.

On this night, I had a mystical land send me her leader to disclose her identity. Do you believe in dreams? In reincarnation? In prophecies? I do, but my question is do you believe a faraway, mystical land is alive and can send her leader to unveil her veil? I had not, but I do after this dream.

This dream is very special as from here, I discovered the name of my favorite country which had come within my dreams throughout my adult life. The veil came off as this country had displayed herself and her name through this dream. All my dreams of being within a faraway land stayed with me for years until one night, a strange dream had come upon my door with a knock from a complete stranger.

My doorbell kept buzzing as I told the buzzer, "Coming! Let me place a leash on my puppy." I rushed and opened my door without looking through the peep hole as I am short and only stand at a height of about five feet and four inches. I can't reach or see through the peep hole. I wanted to change it, but always tomorrow. I am a very small, petite woman, and here as I opened the doors, in front of me I saw standing at over six feet, a complete stranger.

I had strange thoughts go through my mind such as, do not open the door to any strangers, yet I remembered my own quotation, "Strangers are but Angels in disguise."

I said, "Hello. May I help you? Do I know you? Who are you?" He said, "Oh I am Mark, Mark Rutte." I asked, "I never met you?" He said, "No." I asked, "You are a president?"

He said, "Yes, you can call me that. I am a Prime Minister."
I said, "Oh you are Tony Blair, Prime Minister Tony Blair?"

He laughed and said, "No. That was a few years ago. I am
Mark Rutte and I work for the…" I stopped him and said, "You work
for the Queen." He said, "I used to, but now I work for the King.
Prime Minister Mark Rutte."

I know we talked for a long time as he had with him a few
people. I also was shocked to see where I was. I felt like the scenery
was different and I don't recall if I was in my house, a hotel, or
somewhere else. I know it was one of those dreams where you try
hard to remember, what else did we talk about? Why would a
stranger, a Prime Minister be at my door? He probably won't even
remember me, if he had seen me on the road.

I had lived with these questions as I had no clue who Mark
Rutte was. I did, however, remember he introduced himself
repeatedly as, "Mark, Mark Rutte." He had said his first name first
and then repeated it as he said his full name.

As I woke up from this dream, I knew it was a knock upon
my door. I must search for this person. Does he really exist? Is there
a Mark out there? I knew I had a big clue as he had said he was a
Prime Minister. For the first time without fear, I considered my
dreams and did the research. I got the biggest shock, like an
earthquake within my life.

I felt feverish as in front of me on the computer screen, there
was Prime Minister Mark Rutte from the Netherlands. He stands tall
at six feet plus. I do not know the reason of my dream as I know

people will dream of actors and leaders as they connect their imagination to their brain and have what we call daydreams.

Scientific, mystical, and religious theories have analyzed a dream in which you have no connection to the people or places you are dreaming about, as being a message from the beyond. I have done extensive research on dreams and have come to a conclusion. I must be patient for only time will have my answers as I have written about in my Introduction chapter, "Eternal Footprints Through Dreams."

The Netherlands, a country where Mark Rutte is the Prime Minister, has never been on my travel journal as I always thought that I had been to England, so I crossed out Europe as having been there. My travel journal had Paris and Milan listed though if I could afford to go there. The Netherlands was a strange knock upon my door.

Research and history have shown me there were floods in the Netherlands. There is a place called the fisherman's village. There is a port in Rotterdam which was a shock because I saw in another dream that I live in the sister port city of the country that haunts me in my dreams. I live in Seattle, and the sister port city is Rotterdam in the Netherlands.

I don't know how I saw The Prime Minister of the Netherlands, but I know I had seen this country throughout my life. She always had on a veil, and now she finally revealed herself through my blessed dream.

Maybe one day, life will tell me how I saw this dream. In the meantime, I found this leader who I have never met. Through my research, I was inspired by his quotations and the remarkable way he lives his life. Don't fear the past. Don't let fear knock you out. He teaches as he is a teacher and a historian. Without him knowing, he has taught me a lot.

I don't know why I had seen this dream, but after reading about this great leader, I had become a great admirer of this person and I had dedicated two of my books in his name. I had found so much peace within my soul after I found out the identity of this unknown land which is now known through this blessed dream. My dreams from past years have taken pictures within this Earth.

I had searched for this country within different states of my own country. I had gone cross-country throughout the United States, always keeping an eye for this sacred land. Never had I imagined that she is across the ocean in a faraway land.

I know somehow this land had called me like a telephone call from a friend through the miracles of this blessed dream and Prime Minister Mark Rutte. I don't know what the future holds for me and the Netherlands, but I feel like I belong over there and not here. I will let the future guide me as I know The Holy Spirit guides all through the blessed dreams. My prayers shall always be with this land and her children as somehow, I know I have a bond with them and always shall carry this bond within my heart.

My life journey is a wagon filled with struggles from all aspects of life. I take these as a traveler's journey of endurance. Life brings along this path, inspiration from all different corners. My corner was an amazing grace from The Holy Spirit. Through my dreams, I was guided by The Holy Spirit and that path brought me to a stranger, a leader of a small European country. He is known very well for his own journey and simple way of life.

Sometimes in life, a person leaves a great imprint on one's soul, even though you may have never met. In my life, this person was Prime Minister Mark Rutte, who without knowing has inspired this old soul. Now, the land that has come to me through my dreams is alive and breathing in front of me.

I know this land is like the bridge of union for me through miracles as she has called upon me through a blessed soul, the Prime Minister. I had visited the Netherlands before I completed my dream diaries as this whole book was a direct inspiration from this blessed country.

Miracles had been a part of my life, but to have a person from my dreams in front of me even on the computer screen is a miracle. I had not been lucky enough to see the Prime Minister on my visit, but my friends had bumped into him. He was nice and had spoken to them kindly even though he was busy and rushed off.

Life will guide me to wherever she wants to take me. I have complete faith and I know we must do our share to follow the paths laid out to us through the miracles of The Creator. I know the future will guide me as I have complete faith in my Lord.

For all of you, I ask only one thing. Always keep hope alive. At times, when all seem lost and stranded, even then keep holding on to the last strings of hope even if a string is frail and breaking. Hope shall hold on to you as you become frail and give you miracles from beyond. A bridge shall be made through miracles as always from the ocean guiding and watching over us is the Spiritual Lighthouse.

CHAPTER NINE

My Private Grotto

"Throughout the thundering storms of life, through the unknown tsunamis, I hide all my feelings from this world within my own cave, I but call my private grotto."

-Ann Marie Ruby

February 2, 2017

My cave, I love my cave, where I am just myself, where tears are free to fall as they land upon my hands. I don't have to pretend to be anything, but just be myself. I live for peace. I breathe to spread peace, the only motto of life. All my life, I assumed don't see bad, don't talk bad, and don't hear anything bad as no life is without any complication.

I don't want to ever be a public figure as I don't have the courage to be on the stage. I like to see the concert from the perspective of the audience. I admire the world leaders, the artists, and the public figures who but place themselves out there to help the others, to guide the others, or just give the others peace, joy, love, and tears through entertainment. Life seems all glittery and gold, but within their basket of bread, they carry the critics with a big smile, and are always trying to be above the pain.

I know life is complicated, but if we do not walk or do our share, how will all of humanity survive? All my thoughts, and living in my comfortable grotto had changed again with another dream. I was walking in a cave and all around me, different things were going on. I saw I was trying to walk and keep a strong face as I saw obstacles were piling up in front of me.

As I walked, I saw there was a door closing and I knew I must walk out of this cave quickly. I was walking and saw at one corner of the cave, a lot of deaths and disasters, natural and unnatural, were occurring. I was confused as to what was going on.

I saw a lot of ambulances and police officers trying to save different groups of people, all around the world. I knew it was the End of Time and all around there was war.

I saw people were being taken on stretchers. There were people running away from each other. As I was watching this, tears kept on falling. What was going on? I saw houses were being locked up by the occupants and other people who needed help. I knew this was a world I never dreamed of in my life. In my dream, I was crying and I prayed and asked the Heavens above, "What is going on?"

Technology and science have improved as time has passed by, yet morally it seems like we have moved back years. Life is so hard to live. I had grown up with all my doors open and neighbors watching out for each other. Now, technology has improved. The world is but one home, yet we the humans have become even more distanced from each other than ever before. I know people have become estranged over religion, race, and culture. What are the leaders of this world doing?

I heard a voice tell me, "Follow my vehicle." I heard a sports car hitting the break and then pushing the gas pedal. The voice asked me to stop as he hits the break and run as he pushes the gas pedal. I saw I was inside a cave and there were two doors on two sides of the cave. Both doors were open. I had walked into cave through the door that was toward my right-hand side.

As I had entered, I saw there were so many natural and unnatural calamities going on behind that door. I saw known and unknown dead bodies, but I knew I must keep going and not worry about the calamities. I saw a newspaper clipping on the ground of the cave which read, "The prophecies of Nostradamus are coming true." I saw it, but ignored it for I knew I must only deal with the facts and the present for the future only belongs to time. The door in front of me was open, but I did not know why the voice said to wait and follow him. I followed and ran as soon as the gas pedal was pushed.

As I moved forward, behind me a door closed. I was worried and just followed the voice and saw myself walking out of the cave. I then saw four of my closest friends and my puppy were with me. The six of us walked out together, and saw there in front of us was a sports car awaiting our arrival. As the car door opened, a very nice gentleman walked out to let us into his car.

I hugged him and started to cry as I said, "Archangel Michael, you come to visit again." He replied, "Everything shall be okay. Do you have the books with you?"

My friends replied, "Yes, we do. We finally got her to publish the books and now she is out of her cave." I then noticed I had in my hands, a few books. I looked up at all of them and told them I am so nervous to be criticized by humans and not by God. I am not scared of God as I try to live a life within the commandments of my Lord.

I then got a very big hug from The Holy Archangel. We all got into his car as I told him my life goal is for this world to bring back love and harmony within the souls of all humans. I was asked, "And how do you think this is achievable?" I told all, "Through love for oneself and peace for oneself. One must be in peace to spread peace."

My dream broke. This morning, I received a call from my four friends and like always, they all had seen the same dream about my books. I then sat with them and decided it is time I must walk out of the cave. Maybe I can help one person be in peace and spread peace. I published my first book this month. I had published my very special book of prayers and now this is my seventh book, my dream diaries.

Throughout this dream, I had the eerie feeling of where I was and what was going on. I knew we were but living at the End of Time. I knew that is why there was a newspaper article left lying on the cave floor. It was a message from the Heavens above. The End of Time shall come, yet, we all have one question. "When is this to happen?" My answer is as life ends for each person, it is his or her End of Time.

Although unitedly, I see prophecies of seekers from past years are coming true as we are facing a world that has been changed in front of our eyes. We can be the change and hope each individual changes, so collectively we shall have a better world left for the future generations. The seekers have warned us from the past, not to frighten us, but to forewarn us to be safe.

My message for all from this dream is find peace within yourself first for it is then the world shall be in peace. Life is a lesson full of obstacles. I believe all obstacles are but teachers of life, and as we have crossed these obstacles, it is then we have learned our lessons. Let us be there for all the others who but must cross these obstacles. Let us join hands and light the candles for all to follow even during a dark and stormy night. In union, we shall all cross the obstacles and be safe. Let us also appreciate all public figures who are trying to spread peace even though they are being criticized by so many.

Personally, I have written my inspirational quotations, my prayers I call songs, and my dream diaries only to spread peace as I have found peace within them. I am finally out of my grotto where I had found the courage to write and publish my work. Always, I was guided by the Heavens above and by my basic moral values.

If ever you feel lonely, lost, and stranded, know always from the unknown ocean, we are all being guided by the powerful faith of the Spiritual Lighthouse.

CHAPTER TEN

The Voice Of Miracle

"All of you whom have no voice or ways to communicate, I but am always there for you. I am known to you by my birth name called, Miracle."

-Ann Marie Ruby

March 15, 2015

Downtown Seattle, a European style apartment complex with a bakery and Starbucks, the Space Needle within a block was a blessing. I never had a boring day. Rather, days passed by as time seemed to always have her own mind and ways. Smell of fresh baked bread and coffee with tourists always passing by, I felt like I was living in a dreamland. We the humans only live life as The Lord wills and always hope for the best. I always live each day like my prayer, "Life On This Earth Is But A Day."

Each dawn, I open my eyes with my prayer, "Glory Be To My Lord." This was yet another blessed day which at first seemed so scary and within my lips I had repeated, "Not again my Lord."

I have complete faith The Lord always keeps the hidden blessings even within all hurdles. So, I live my life with caution and blessings. The night came with the feeling of spring knocking around the corner, yet I wanted to enjoy the last few days of winter. Nature and her true beauty always strike a chord within my soul. Again, I had miracles placed upon my door as sleep came within my mind and body.

I saw I was walking with Patches, my puppy. He seemed very tired and refused to walk as he was falling asleep. I asked Patches what was going on and why is he not running or barking at the strangers.

Then, I saw my puppy dropped his head and was falling asleep in the road. I asked him, "What is it baby?" Suddenly, in front of me, my puppy fell dropping his head and just fell asleep. I tried to wake him up, but he was not moving. I panicked and knew Patches needed to go to a doctor immediately. I saw someone urging me to take him to the doctor urgently.

After this dream as I had awakened, I made an emergency visit with my puppy's doctor. I always have my fear of letting anyone know I am here because I just had a dream, but told the doctor I am really worried about Patches because I just have a bad feeling. The veterinarian was very kind and checked Patches. The doctors came out and said they would need to do more tests as they were worried why no one noticed he might have bladder stones.

Without thinking, I asked how it was even possible because Patches had just had a physical. I know life is a search engine where we search for everything until our last breath and even then, we don't have the answers.

The doctor told me Patches had bladder stones and needed to go through a surgery. The doctor was shocked how I had brought Patches in as he had not cried or shown any of the symptoms before we came. Patches was in a lot of pain and started to bleed as he was brought in. The surgery went well as I brought Patches home.

Dreams are messages from the Heavens above always to guide us through the obstacles of life. Keep an eye out for the messages given to you through your dreams for had I ignored this message, the situation could have been very different. Life is full of hurdles, but then life is a blessing as The Lord always keeps an eye out for us through miracles.

The doctor had asked me how was I able to detect the problem as that is why Patches is now healed. It was a very hard time for my puppy and it was even harder for me as he could not communicate with me through the terms known to us as words or actions. I would think he would have cried and had other symptoms. I guess he did, but as always, he was happy with his treats and his playtime or just being cuddled.

I guess sometimes, we the humans too go through this type of problem and for me, I always turn to my Lord when and where there is help or no help. I had turned to the doctors as The Lord has sent them to heal all creation. I know for me always at the break of dawn, I shall always pray on my knees to my Lord, my Creator.

For me personally, today I was again guided by the Heavens above through another dark night where all but get lost. My message for all of whom but knock, seek, and ask, know this truth within all things of life. The messages from the Heavens above should never be ignored. Miracles do happen. Have faith always and never lose faith for hold on to her even when she seems so far away.

For all of you whom are but seeking the spiritual path, do believe and know that throughout all the darkness, glowing above the ocean, always standing tall as she guides all lost and stranded is the Spiritual Lighthouse.

CHAPTER ELEVEN

War Within The Heavens Above, Earth Beneath

"War begins within each soul as we create an army of good, versus all evil."

-Ann Marie Ruby

May 11, 2012

Life is a miracle where we live our complete life thinking about our existence on Earth. How did we arrive upon this Earth? We the humans welcome dawn as she breaks through the night's sky to only glorify the days. We await the night's sky as we light up the lanterns to help us throughout the dark nights. I watch mothers burning their hands to keep the candles burning throughout the dark times.

I watch lighthouses all across this Earth filling up their oil lanterns, so they can guide the lost and stranded to safety. As the night skies brighten up with the moon shining from the skies up in Heaven, I know Angels are but watching over us for eternity. I had an amazing dream this night, a topic I was not even aware existed within my knowledge as I had never thought of it to be possible.

Within this dream, I carried within myself fear and only one thought—I must survive. I had been running for my life as the fear of rape and murder gripped my soul. I had a baby within my womb, but I spoke with my child as I ran. I felt that was my only comfort for as I touched my womb, I felt my child and my husband with me. A man was chasing after me, wanting to rape me. Somehow, I knew there was a woman with him too. I thought the woman was even more ferocious than the man.

I managed to somehow injure him and buy time. I knew he was easier to handle further away from her. I kept running as the man said, "Since you are family, I will give you a head start. If you can go, then I'll leave you alone. But, if I catch you, I'll see." I kept saying, "Oh my Lord, help me! Oh, The Holy Archangels of Heaven, please help!" I knew some of my friends were also running as a war had broken out and all the people were running from the beast.

My only thought was I must find my husband somehow, but where and how? I must save my child and then find my husband. I knew the beast was after my family. I had to save my children, my husband, and my friends. I entered a square shaped jungle and the beast turned around as if he would not look for thirty minutes to give me a head start.

That was not a head start because it would really take him just two minutes to come to me. He was a giant and I was so small it would take me much longer to run because of the height difference. I knew I had helped all of whom I could help on the way. As I had the beast running after me, I prayed.

In the jungle, someone quietly grabbed my arm and did not speak or make a sound. I did not know if this person was male or female. This person moved a finger to his or her lips signaling me to be quiet and gave me a blue shawl. I thought this person was hiding in something and was helping me secretly and quietly. With the blue shawl, I was invisible.

I asked, "Where is Archangel Michael? Why is he not here yet?" I heard the Heavens had sounded a warning of some kind, "Archangel Michael has declared a War in Heaven. He shall rescue all of God's army and the creation with all The Archangels. As all of God's creation but jump onto Earth, they forget everything. Please do remember as much as you can, for the War in Heaven continues on Earth." I told the voice, "I will forever belong only to The Omnipotent and I shall fight to bring the children back home. All the children of God shall return home safely. Let this war on Earth begin."

I saw so many people jumping onto Earth. I felt fear gripping within my soul as I cried, "My Lord may I never go astray and never fall prey to the beast. In whatever form or shape I may turn out to be, may I only be Your true devotee." I knew all the humans must jump through the river of life and begin their journey.

I also knew the beast hides within the oceans of this world, and Archangel Michael shall declare a War on Earth against the beast at the End of Time. Without any hesitation, I jumped onto Mother Earth for protection saying, "Mother Earth, swallow me!" I began my journey.

My dream had broken as I had shivers within my soul and I did not know what to expect from this dream. I searched again for proof and this time I found proof from all over the world, from all different religions, races, and time zones. I also got two messages from this Earth on two different days.

My friends had called and made me aware of their interlinking dreams of running away from the beast. I had met up with a pastor who was visiting with his wife who said she too had a running away from Heaven dream where she knew there were so many people running with her. She had nonstop childhood nightmares as she was growing up because of these dreams.

I had forgotten all about it and had been visiting Downtown Seattle. I was at the Macy's store for a break as I love shopping. A stranger had stopped me and I had a strange encounter with this stranger, who had just said, "So Ann Marie, how does it feel to be back from Heaven?" I was shocked how he knew my name, not in his question.

I walked past him without uttering a word, but the words stayed with me. I believe in reincarnation and that life is a circle, but also believe this life has been given so we complete the circle, not let the circle complete us. Change what has been wronged and not be wronged. Some words linger on and just stay with you forever, for me these words of a stranger.

I don't know if this stranger was an Angel in disguise, but his words coming after my dream gave me a strange feeling that I would not want to describe with any words. I do not believe any words would justify these feelings.

I have personally done a lot of research and know within the Bible and other texts, there are stories about running from Heaven although they differ in languages and religious groups. Yet, within a lot of voices around the globe, people are testifying to the facts of having dreams about running away from the beast. I know through our journey of life, however, we are running away from him within every day of our lives. With complete faith, I know no one can harm us as we only have to keep our faith within The Lord, The Omnipotent.

The reason for this dream, I believe may be to show this is how we the humans ended up on Earth. As we ran from the beast through the rivers of life, we were reborn and picked up by our life journey upon Earth. As I have written within the last chapter of my dream diaries, I do have a dream in which people were arriving on boats through the river of life. At the end of their lives, they again take a boat back to the river of life.

From my various dreams, I believe the dragon, the beast, the serpent, or whatever name he is known by, lives within this ocean of life as he tries to take all astray. Within that same dream, I did see The Holy Archangels guiding and watching over all from the glass house within the ocean where The Omnipotent awaits and watches all the children as they are brought to and from the Earth to this miraculous place where all the miracles but take place. I had called this place as all The Archangels had also called this place, the Spiritual Lighthouse.

CHAPTER TWELVE

Soul To Soul From The Heavens Above To Earth Beneath

"Sacred union between soulmates, is but the eternal bliss of life. Nothing exists but the two, a man and a woman, whom God has but created for each other. Within this holy union everything is but complete."

-Ann Marie Ruby

February 2, 2013

Night dawns upon us, as she reminds all it is now dark and we must survive until dawn breaks open. It's how we struggle through this period that takes us to dawn. Fear holds us back from always confronting the truth. This fear is the fear of being questioned, or being ridiculed, or just being afraid of this unknown term called fear.

I love to wait for the night to turn around and become dawn as some nights I lie within my bed and watch the night sky turn to dawn. I compare this struggle with fighting for our beliefs and what is rightfully ours. I have always been the one who but gives up, even though I know I was right. Why fight and have bad breath? Just keep it inside and move on. That was me until I knew I must stop and awaken myself before it is too late.

I believed in arranged marriages, no divorce, or just never be the one to express your personal feelings. I now know it is wrong to be forced into a relationship where there is no union of the mind, body, and soul. In these cases, divorce is a blessing for how can there be a union complete within the mind, body, and soul if the two joined in union are but wrong for each other? How does one know or how do you take the right step and not be criticized by the society?

I knew I must stop thinking of what others but think. I must let go of all my inner fears and just be free from all obstacles that are but placed within my walk of life. My thought always was to keep my feelings buried within my chest, so there is peace on Earth.

Every day, I would imagine all my personal feelings be buried like a dead person, being buried within the Earth, so there is peace on Earth. I realized I was hurting myself by burying myself with all the burdens of mixed cultural concepts. I realized there are no cultural concepts where the mind, body, and soul are involved, but personal feelings and personal conception. Set the mind, body, and soul free to feel.

Let there be love in the soul, not understanding and compromise, but freedom of the mind, body, and soul. Do not compromise your soul for the wrong reason. Loving The Lord comes from complete freedom of one's own mind, body, and soul. Falling in love with one's complete soulmate should be from the inner mind, body, and soul. I love my Lord without knowing or seeing or hearing the voice, but with just complete faith. Love between soulmates should be the same. Otherwise, it is just a compromise. Sometimes, you must be hurt and disappointed to enter this spiritual realm.

This night, I had a spiritually awakening dream. Within this night, I had energized all my thoughts and beliefs as I know with this newly found belief, I must walk on this path of soulmate love and understanding, all with a candle in my hand. With complete faith, I walk and I do not let anyone compromise my own feelings or faith. For now, I just hold on to the candles of hope. I had tried to stay awake and watch dawn this night, but my body gave up and sleep had taken over my mind and body as this night, I had a very sacred dream.

As I was walking across a delta region, I saw a huge crowd of people gather at the river bank. I asked an elderly gentleman what was going on. Why have all the people gathered around the river bank? I saw the elderly gentleman smile at my words as he asked me, "Where have you come from? Your mother tongue is different from ours." I understood they were talking in a different language, yet I understood everything, and he understood me. He seemed so familiar, but I could not quite understand where I had seen him. I waited with the crowd as I thought these people had gathered here for a long period of time and were just watching something in the river.

I heard the crowd kept on repeating, "How long will he stay asleep? Won't he drown?" I then followed the crowd's gaze and saw within the river, there was a man sleeping on top of a boat, or a huge flower, or something that looked like a raft. He was floating on top of it as he had no care. He lay asleep and was at risk. Somehow, I was so worried for him as my world had frozen in front of me.

I asked the crowd, "How long has he been sleeping on top of that thing?" The man answered, "For years he has been asleep and just floating." I asked, "Then, why are all of you afraid for him? He has been safe for this long. Why would he be at risk now?"

The man answered, "It is time he must awaken as now all the dangers of life will affect him. The water shall rise. The rivers have been filled with snake poison and if the water touches him, it shall be risky. The poison of the snakes shall be all over the water, and if he does not awaken, then he will never awaken but be poisoned."

I asked them, "Why don't you all help him? Just go and wake him up." They said they cannot, for only his soulmate can awaken him from his sleep. They must meet and as they meet, he shall awaken from his sleep. I asked the elderly man, "What happens if he is not awakened and the water rises?" The man replied, "All shall end."

I did not know what he meant by the words "all shall end," but I got scared for the man sleeping so calmly. I knew my soul wanted to do something, anything. I started to walk toward the water. The crowd screamed not to go near the water as it has been poisoned and if touched, all shall end. I knew the poison shall kill me too, but I felt like my soul cried for this man. I do not know if it was just humanity or something more as I felt the pull and I could not keep my feet steady on the ground.

I felt like even if I did not move, my feet started to walk and my hands started to wave toward him. I cried and told them, "But how can I let a human be in danger? I will never be able to forgive myself if I stood there and just watched." I started to run as the elderly man grabbed me and told me, "Do not be foolish. Do you not care for yourself?"

I told him, "Strangely, I feel like I won't even exist if I don't go to him now." I watched the elderly man as he kept watching me. I knew I must do something and run from this crowd. I watched the elderly man now had placed a walking stick in front of him. I planned to grab his walking stick, so I could stop the people from preventing me to go into the poisonous river.

I told them, "I just need to hold on to something as I have traveled thousands of miles on my feet and need to rest." The elderly man gave me his walking stick to hold. I watched him as he smiled at me. I thought of Moses and how he had crossed the river for God. I knew I shall cross this snake river for God's creation. May the blessings be upon me. I took his walking stick and ran toward the water. No one followed me. I told all I don't know why but I must save him. I feel like I have no life without him and I must go to him at any cost. Even if I must cross this snake river, I shall.

I walked into the snake poisoned water and I knew my feet just walked and never asked for my permission, nor did my hands, my eyes, or even my body who had her own will. I prayed to my Lord for help as the water was burning my skin. I felt shivers all over my body and I knew I must somehow make it to him.

I tried to awaken the man from his sleep as I screamed at the top of my voice for him to be awakened, yet he was sleeping with all the calmness this world could give him. I knew, however, he too was not in peace. He was asleep, but sad and he looked like he too waited for something within this poisoned river. I worried about the warnings given by the elderly gentleman as he had warned only his soulmate can awaken him.

The man kept on screaming, "Only his soulmate will fill his soul with her soul. They are made for each other. The two make one. They will complete each other when they but unite from two to one."

As I ignored all the warnings coming to me from all different corners, I kept on swimming as if my life depended on it. I climbed over on top of the raft and as I touched the man's hand, his hands had clapped on to mine. A button had clicked, and he opened his eyes. I was scared now what?

My heart started to beat faster as I felt his hands on my hands. I knew these hands. I saw his eyes and knew his eyes. I had seen them repeatedly. As I had walked with The Holy Archangels, I had seen him, and I knew at once who he was.

He opened his mouth as he spoke, "Ann Marie Ruby, you came! I have been waiting for you as I have meditated and gone into complete mind, body, and soul meditation. Yet, I know you shall come and awaken me."

I told him, "How can I not come to my soulmate? If you are not awake, then I must awaken you for soulmates must unite. Why have you not awakened? It is so hard for me to fight this battle all alone within this poisoned water." I cried and retold my life story to him. As I wept all over him, he just watched me. I held on to him and knew at all cost, I will save him and never let him go or let him be in any harm's way.

I saw the crowd on the shore all turned into Angels as they were saying you will awaken him, we promise you. I watched the elderly gentleman laugh and say, "Whatever it takes, you must be strong and know you have the blessings of the Heavens above."

He said, "In life, people unite with the wrong person and the union turns into a divorce. Know then, it was the wrong person. If you are not married and you think that's it, life for you is to be a single, know that he or she awaits your arrival. Faith is believing not questioning."

Life is a miracle filled with blessings. I watched Archangel Michael smiling as he said, "Remember soul to soul, you can awaken him." I knew Archangel Michael smiling from far away was a message of peace for me. I wished I had The Holy Angels here around me as my sleep had broken. My dream had broken as I saw my pillows had been drenched yet again with teardrops.

I knew that within this dream, a lot of mythological stories had been hidden. After seeing the dream, I had researched this topic for a long time and saw a lot of cultures talk about soulmates and the union of soulmates. I knew I was not in any rush for I have given my mind, body, and soul to my Lord. But, I also knew I must not be afraid of the poisoned river and have faith. If he is asleep, I shall awaken him for I know this world is blessed and we have The Blessed Angels walking all around us like strangers in disguise.

For all of you, my message is never give up on anything in life because of fear. Do not let fear take the last victory, but always wipe off fear with faith and complete belief in The Omnipotent. Hold on to the hands of hope and faith as they shall cross you over the poisonous river of life, to the eternal river of truth.

After I had seen so many dreams about soulmates I have included some interesting facts about soulmates for all of you seeking the peace of mind from different religious views.

Judaism talks in detail about soulmates. I have one such example that proves The Creator has chosen soulmates from the Heavens above even before birth.

In the Babylonian Talmud, it is stated,

"But Rav Yehudah said: Rav said Forty days before the formation of a fetus a Heavenly voice emanates and says, 'The daughter of so-and-so [will be matched] to so-and-so, the house of so-and-so to so-and-so, the field of so-and-so to so-and-so'" ("Sotah" 2a:9).

In the Zohar, "Each soul and spirit prior to its entering into this world, consists of a male and female united into one being. When it descends on this earth the two parts separate and animate two different bodies. At the time of marriage, the Holy One, blessed be He, who knows all souls and spirits, unites them again as they were before, and they again constitute one body and one soul, forming as it were the right and left of one individual" ("Qabbalah Page").

I believe we the creation but get disconnected with our soulmates as we get engaged within the sin of this world. Therefore, we don't always find our soulmate.

Like the following song of King Solomon, I pray we also find our soulmates, "It was but a little that I passed from them, but I found him whom my soul loveth" (*King James Version*, Song of Solomon 3:4).

Within Hinduism, I found my personal belief that soulmates must be connected mind to mind, body to body, and soul to soul. In Hinduism, we can see the soulmate term within the "Ardhanarishvara" which is also known by the term Shiv Shakti. The God Shiva and his consort The Goddess Parvati represent the left and right sides of one whole individual. The Ardhanarishvara depicts the union of the male God and the female Goddess. They are incomplete without each other, but when in union, they have all the masculine and feminine energies of the universe, forming the perfect bond of soulmates.

The concept of soulmates uniting is also mentioned in the Bible as follows. "And they twain shall be one flesh: so then they are no more twain, but one flesh" (*King James Version*, Mark 10:8).

I personally believe we the humans, because of cultural and personal infatuations, fall into the trap of our own sins and ruin the path we were destined to follow by The Omnipotent. We see even to this day within some countries, arranged marriages are made and couples are sometimes united with their soulmates. Yet, some are united with the biggest misery of life and end in divorces, and in these cases, lose hope to unite with soulmates. My message is don't ever lose hope for you have until your last breath.

For all of you whom are thinking within your mind, "But how do I achieve this victory?" Know watching over all of you and guiding all throughout eternity, from the dark ocean is always the Spiritual Lighthouse.

CHAPTER THIRTEEN

The Future Calling From Afar

"The present is but here to steady our mind, body, and soul, for all the unseen, unknown future that is yet to come upon our shore."

-Ann Marie Ruby

July 1, 2016

Life is a mystery lived within mysteries. All is known, but also unknown to this mind, body, and soul. Knowledge is but the answer to all mysteries solved. Living in Seattle, Washington is a blessing as even within the roads of Downtown Seattle, we get to witness mysteries within our existence.

The Farmers' Market in Downtown Seattle is an amazing place to be in as you can walk through the history of the Pike Place Market. You can spend the whole day there, yet you would still want more time to be with her.

From Downtown Seattle to Downtown Tacoma, all by the Puget Sound, the Cascades stand tall, giving all her residents an amazing view to escape from the obstacles of daily life. I love living here and feel lucky to have my Lord's blessings within these wonders of life.

I had another beautiful night where the crescent moon was visible. I give my gratitude to the artist, my Creator for this amazing picturesque art. I sat outside on my deck, watching the ferry boats cross over to the islands. I always love the feeling of knowing that these ferry boats have someone's beloved waiting to go home, maybe with warm dinner waiting on the table with loved ones watching over. I prayed may all people be safe and reach their homes safely. May all couples find comfort within their true love. May a mother be able to comfort her children within a warm blanket of hugs.

I turned in bed and from my bedroom, I had a spectacular view of the Puget Sound and all the islands. The stars were sparkling their beautiful glitter all over the water. I knew I was blessed and prayed as I watched the beautiful view through my windows. Sleep, however, took over and my dream followed.

I saw I was walking with him again. I knew him in my dreams and life was complete with him. I again saw walking with us were The Archangels. I don't know if The Archangels were visible to all or just me. The Archangels were walking with me by the Puget Sound, which I kept calling an ocean. They told me, "Watch. This is where the bridge will be made." I asked, "How?" They said, "It shall be and all shall be done. Have faith."

I knew I saw my husband, my soulmate, as he too knew we were together, yet somehow not together. I knew I had walked with a lot of people. As I saw The Angels had placed something in the water, I asked, "What have you placed in the water?" They said, "Watch."

I saw with a pen in their hands were The Holy Angels, all glowing as they placed the pen within the water and there in front of us appeared a bridge. I walked over the bridge and there I was with him, my soulmate. The Angels said, "Watch. Where are you?" I answered, "I am in the Netherlands, the land of Prime Minister Mark Rutte. He had come to visit and told me the name of this mystical land within my dreams, and all of my dreams of this mystical land is not a mystery anymore."

They said, "Leaders are God's blessings and whatever the humans may think, God always has a hand in choosing the leaders of a nation. Yes, at times all get contaminated by the beast, but some leaders are chosen by The Creator."

I saw then we were walking to our house and we were alone now. Within my dream, I was not even shocked as I knew this place so well. We referred to the house as the lake house. There was a river behind us and two roads that went to the house. The house was at the corner of the two roads. There was a lot of privacy around the house. In front of the house, there was a lake and we had a beach near the house.

I knew even in my dream, we were both witnessing this miracle within our dreams. I prayed and asked The Holy Spirit for guidance as I know these are miracles from the Heavens above and most of my dreams do come true except I know some have taken so long. I always have faith in my Lord and I know all is The Lord's will. I kept praying may my Lord's will always prevail, as I wanted some proof of my dream to keep my faith intact and never may I go astray or be upon the wrong path.

Again, The Archangels appeared and told me, "Remember this land is but the sister port city of the city you had rented your apartment in."

As morning came rushing to my doors, I had forgotten about the dream. My friend had visited that night and told me she had seen in her dream, I had moved overseas to the Netherlands. I told her about my dream as she got on the computer and what waited for us on the internet was shocking. It said, one of the sister port cities of Seattle is Rotterdam in the Netherlands.

I told my friend not to get excited as there are a lot of sister port cities and dreams should be miracles and guides of life. I believe we should never jump upon a boat to cross the ocean until we know the boat and the ocean are safe to travel upon. Also, the place you go to must always be safe and awaiting your arrival. I am always fearful of knocking on a door that never opens. My friend, however, told me to knock first and see if it opens.

With her advice upon my door, I promised I will never close the doors to any openings, but I will only travel upon the path of my Lord and with my Lord's guidance. If it is The Lord's will, then the path shall be made and the boat shall come to carry me over.

The message from my dream is that I know we are shown these miracles to be guided by and not to lose hope or fall prey to disappointments or any depression of life. Life is full of miracles and blessings. Never lose hope and always know if a door closes, another one opens with the blessings of The Lord. I wondered about all my dreams and thought why does the Netherlands keep coming to me and what is the message I must take from her.

I still have not decided as I know if I had Moses or my Lord here walking with me over the waters, I would go blindly. This life, however, is filled with obstacles and I must wait for the bridge to appear before I cross any ocean. So, I must be patient for time is my bridge, and may my prayers always lead me to honor, justice, and courage.

I believe in guidance from the future for within The Omnipotent, all is but today, not yesterday or tomorrow. Time is but a zone for we the humans. Live life to the best of your ability. Avoid sins and any sinful acts as they are but the blockages and hurdles of life. Within a blessed life even if all but seem dark and lost, there is hope for within the deep lost ocean, watching over all of us is but the Spiritual Lighthouse.

CHAPTER FOURTEEN

The Flood From The Past

"Time is a blessing for as she travels by us, she collects memories from the present, gives them to the past, and stores them for us to find as a treasure chest in the future."

-Ann Marie Ruby

June 24, 2016

Time is a capsule prescribed to us with the right dosage for our individual bodies. The knowledge of time is with us through the historical facts of the past. The future is unknown and the past is but common knowledge through the diaries of the past. Dreams and miracles, however, are always in the present as The Lord gives us knowledge from the future and the past within the dreams of miracles.

I have had miracles happen to me through dreams as I was guided to be at a place for a job interview or doctor's office for prevention. I have also been foretold of other miracles that take place all around me. I had seen the election results or other future activities to take place within my dreams before they really happened. I was able to write them down and share with only my close friends.

What about the past? What happens to the people who have left us or the places they love and have left behind? What happens after death? Miracles have knocked upon my door as I have had visitors from the world of the dead. They were always peaceful souls saying their farewell or trying to send a message from the other world to their loved ones. I have tried to pass on messages to the families, but it is hard when I really don't want to leave my comfortable cave and be exposed as a psychic who can see only what The Lord wills for me to see within my dreams. Am I a psychic or just a vehicle for The Lord? We all are but a vehicle and we only can see what The Lord wills.

This was a blessed night where I had a date with a handsome man from the past. The dream started off as I was walking within a town. I had no clue where it was, but something bad was going to happen and I knew I must save some people as somehow, they will be related to me in the future.

I walked and ran as fast as I could, trying to warn people to be safe. I knew some of these people I will never meet, but my future generations are because of these people being able to live through the ordeal they must go through today. The town felt like a movie set and time was brought back by the magic of the silver screen like an old Hollywood movie set where life was different and simple.

I saw farmers, farmhouses, and lands that were in a flood-prone delta area. I knew I must warn the people something bad is coming and with the forewarning, a lot of lives will be saved. The future of a lot of people depended on this.

I saw men running all around as the warning was going on and people were trying to get their boats to run away. I stopped and talked with a kind gentleman who was helping all the people go into attics and onto boats. He looked like a very kind-hearted man who was so busy, he forgot his own wife. She had no worries. With all smiles, she was serving everyone drinks and boiled eggs.

I knew people were very polite and were not worried, but I knew I must save him for from him, comes the future of my family. I ran and saw a very kind-hearted young couple and children walking onto a boat. I told them to be careful and safe. I asked them to take all the children and go to the fisherman's village. I heard the people kept repeating the word, "Marken" and I kept repeating to them, "I will meet you at the fisherman's village."

I saw a man whispered amongst themselves, "Who is she? How did she appear with a boat? And where did she go?" Someone else said, "Oh don't bother. She is a beautiful woman and I am a handsome man." I laughed and hugged him as I said, "Only if we could meet, but I won't be born in your time." He had a young son and maybe more children with him, but I just saw the young boy and knew he too would be related to me in the future. I also knew I would not meet them as time was not going to help us. I knew they said the year was 1916.

I kissed his head and thought whoever is your son or grandson or granddaughter is a lucky child to have you. I knew this family would go through a lot, but they would be strong and just fine. I walked with this kind man all night as we walked by the river. He had told me his name and his son's name, but I knew somehow, he was a grandfather figure. He had known it too as he said, "I know we won't meet, but I will leave a family Bible with my grandson, and you will find it safe within the family."

I had numerous dreams with this kind-hearted gentleman whom I know so well, yet as I awaken from my sleep, I know he is still in the past as I am in the present. Within my dream, I knew in between us we had the obstacle of time for the wagon of time would pass by and I would not meet neither the father nor the son. I had seen them repeatedly and know they are blessed as they have the blessings of The Lord with them.

I am glad to know people have kind-hearted grandparents and I am lucky to read about them. In this way, I too live through their stories and we all who do not have a family, have one family through the kind stories that are reported on the news. I prayed may there be kind-hearted families who accept all race, color, and religion as one family.

As I had awakened from my sleep, I had again opened the computer to research about floods and 1916. I knew this time from my dream, I had a few clues. I knew the year, the name of the town Marken, and a fisherman's village. I also have the names of the grandfather and the father who were walking with me. I have kept them private as only time will tell me in the future if I have some connection with them. I knew within my dreams, time would not allow us to meet, but I would somehow meet their future generation.

To my wonders, there comes in my view the flood of 1916 in the Netherlands, in Marken, and yes there is a place called the fisherman's village. I was in a shock as to why I had seen this dream for as far as I know, I don't have any relatives from Europe or the Netherlands. I thought about the people and the life of an old European city. I also remembered there was a lot of wood work and I remembered wooden swings. Fish was also a way of life. I knew they had dairy farms and were worried about livestock.

My research had told me there was loss of life, but thank The Lord, not as much as there could have been. I felt peace and comfort within my chest for the family I had visited in my dream was safe. Is this not strange that my tears betrayed me today, as I broke down crying for a grandfather I had never known or a father that I had never met?

In 1988, I had a dream in which I had seen a grandfather and a father were sitting on a tree and the father fell off. I cried as I had asked, "What just happened?" I heard The Lord reply, "The father who had waited for you for so long has passed away." I had been in New Orleans at the time and had shared the story with a lot of friends. I was young and never paid any mind to it. After this dream, I knew these pure souls come to visit me somehow.

I guess even after death, the souls live on and The Lord can do miracles from anywhere. I knew The Lord had shown me this dream for a very special reason only known by the future. For me, I was just happy knowing a family was safe and they have in their family tree, names of their father, mother, children, grandchildren, and great grandchildren.

It gave me a peace of mind that I cannot explain with words. I guess when you don't have much of a family, it feels so nice to see a family tree safe which shall continue to be safe throughout the future. How am I related to this family, I don't know, but I feel like the future is just that, the future. The past is just that, the past, and all we have today is the present.

It is a gift to all of us to save our combined future. Let us live it in harmony and always remember there is a family member you do not know about who has adopted you as family and shall always pray for you, not for anything but for this bond of union that is created from true love.

As always, my message to all of you is do not ever give up on anything. Always keep hope alive. The Lord is always watching over us as miracles happen throughout time and tide. Water washes over land as she unites the ocean and the lands. My teardrops fall and unite the past, present, and future. If there is even one family out there, we all have a future. Families are not always made from blood, but I believe through love.

This blessed dream had revived my complete faith in all race, color, and religion as my belief is strong as ever and that is, we are all but bonded into one family through the blessed word, love.

For all the lost and stranded souls looking out for hope, faith, and love, always know she is out there waiting for you to open the doors. Like always, from the deep, dark ocean watching over us is the Spiritual Lighthouse.

CHAPTER FIFTEEN

Journey To The Unknown

"What may seem like a nightmare turns out to be a blessed dream only after we have but awakened from our deep sleep."

-Ann Marie Ruby

November 3, 2013

Lincoln City, Oregon, on a cross-country vacation. Now with all honesty, it was a one-time, very courageous event I really don't think I would do again. I left everything behind and went on a vacation with some of my friends.

I had placed my house in Arizona up for sale, and moved into a vacation house. I then bought a recreational vehicle and went on a tour across the country. Life had given me obstacles and pain to live with, but I know with the blessings of my Lord, I survived. This was a cold, wet, and drizzling night. We had parked our RV and the SUV in a vacation RV park, in Lincoln City, Oregon, a small and quiet city with so many views to enjoy. I loved the oceanfront villas and resorts. I went and saw a small house built in 1900. I fell in love with the house and had decided to buy the property.

My life though always has her own choice and decides for me what I should avoid and where to go and how to go. The rain in Lincoln City, Oregon is always a companion as it comes and leaves, but keeps on giving us the gift of her presence. The RV was very nice. As I had never been in one, I was worried about the rain, but it was a blessing as I saw firsthand how RV living feels.

For some people, this has become what they want in life and it's just perfect for them. Our RV had a full kitchen, a very nice bathroom, a bedroom with a queen bed, and a separate living quarter that had sleeping arrangement for another six people.

I had the privilege to have the private bedroom, as all my friends knew I am a single woman who lives a sacred life. All my friends are very spiritual and a blessing for me.

We all had a quiet night as the following dream had visited me. I was walking in a downtown city where people were sightseeing around a tower looking structure. I saw I was walking with a very familiar person. He walked with me for a very long time as I asked him, "Where am I?" He said, "Seattle." I said, "I have never been to Seattle." He asked, "May I have a hug?"

I hugged him as I knew him so well. We walked to a library nearby and saw the Farmers' Market. We walked for a long time. I asked, "Who are you and why do I know you so well?" That's when a light appeared in front of us and I knew The Holy Spirit had started to talk to me from the light as He said, "Move to Seattle. Your house is there." I knew this was strange as I don't know anyone in Seattle and have never been to Seattle. I saw a huge library and a big greenhouse type of place we walked into. I walked past so many buildings all night.

I knew all night, I must go to Seattle. I awoke to another strange morning as I felt lonely, but I love The Holy Spirit more than my life and knew if there is any message in this dream, then I must follow. I shall not rush with haste as I will let God guide me through this.

I always share my dreams with everyone, but I thought how do I share this dream. I am about to buy a house in Lincoln City,

Oregon and start a new life in a beachfront chalet from 1900 with all the modern luxury and spectacular view of the Pacific Ocean.

A knock upon our RV door was shocking as on a vacation, you don't get visits from vacationers. An elderly gentleman came to the door and said he was from Arizona too and wanted to say hi. We spoke for a while as he said he does not know how to say this, but he saw a dream in which The Holy Spirit had visited him and gave him a message, to let Ann know she will be fine and always know The Lord watches over all as the only thing we need is faith.

He gave us fruits he had brought on his trip from his garden and gave us his address to keep in touch. There was another event from that morning. After the gentleman left, one of my friends said she saw in her dream, we were driving over a bridge called 520. There were graves of Native Americans under that bridge. She saw Archangel Michael had sent her a message saying, "Move to Seattle."

That morning, we all opened our friend Google and in front of our eyes, Seattle stood as it did in my dream from last night. It was shocking to see the details of the dream on the map. On top of it, my friend was having goosebumps as we found out the 520 Bridge was built over Native American grave sites.

I must say it was a very blessed morning as I had decided I would follow the dreams and go to Seattle. Whatever life might keep in store for me, I shall face, but I knew the answer to my question was time. Be patient as time is a bridge we all cross only once and when and where we have guidance from The Lord, we must comply.

So, we all decided whatever life has in store, Seattle here we come. Sometimes in life, we make mistakes and do what is wrong or the path we choose might not be correct, but sometimes we just try our best and let the miracles of life take over with complete faith.

Decisions we took were not in favor of our future. Financially, work wise, and physically, it was draining all of us. For me personally, it was a very trying period of my life. I was searching for a quiet place to retire. Yes, I knew people laughed why was I thinking of retiring at an early age. Life is a journey and age is but a perception of the mind. I know I am but the owner of an old soul. My wisdom of life is simple—do the right thing and always live within the basic moral values as your guide.

I followed my dream of that night and had moved to Seattle. Even though it was hard and trying at times, I never lost faith in my Lord. With complete faith, we are but able to cross all the bridges of obstacles. I have always kept the candles of hope glowing within my heart and for all the stranded obstacles of life. Faith had been my partner throughout the journey of my life.

The move to Seattle and the struggles within Seattle were hard-earned transitions, but a blessing in disguise because I love living in Seattle. The person in my dreams who always shows up when I am in danger or need help, I call my guiding Angel. I know he is my soulmate guiding me from afar. I have complete faith I will meet him one day, as my dreams are a guidebook through my life.

My friends moved with me as all of them found jobs in Seattle and everyone loves this city. The Lord is merciful as we were all blessed to be able to do this financially and physically. More dreams and guidance continued throughout our lives within Seattle. Miracles had taken course as I had been blessed with more dreams guiding my friends to their employers and housing and all throughout, we held on to the hands of faith. We always had within our basket, basic moral values and wisdom of life to guide us.

Life is a journey within a journey where we have obstacles all around us. I believe as always, obstacles are but teachers of life. As we have crossed them, we have learned our lesson. Also remember from the unknown, unseen, always guiding us throughout this journey of life is the Spiritual Lighthouse.

CHAPTER SIXTEEN

Visit From The Archangels, Vatican City

"Messages come from the unknown as a guiding light for all of humanity."

-Ann Marie Ruby

August 6, 2012

I was in Arizona at the time and had bought a white ranch house with five acres of land. I loved the cute small ranch house and thought again, this is it. Never moving again. At least that was the plan. Summer in Arizona was an experience of a lifetime. It was very hot and humid. I had walked during the summer nights as it cooled down after a very hot day. I lived right off Route 66 in a golf course community.

There were antique shops and tourist shops all around the quiet town. During the nights, I had to walk with a big walking stick as I was warned about the coyotes and rattlesnakes. This was Arizona desert life with a small ranch house surrounded by mountains and nothing else in sight. All the houses were quite far from each other. No neighbor would drop by even in an emergency. I had to keep enough groceries and emergency supplies as the nearest grocery store was about an hour drive.

Most of the houses were solar powered. I had public power and was on septic and well water. I loved it and dreamed of going solar. It was a simple life where I could hear the cows and dogs and all other animals from faraway houses. The stars were so clear and I could breathe fresh air from the mountains. I had a stream running through my property and the sound of the water was mesmerizing.

After a long walk, I still felt like something was missing. I wondered if all of this was too quiet for me. I love living in a secluded neighborhood where I could be left alone to do as I wish, but somehow, I also want to know if my neighbors are all okay. I want to know if anyone is sick or if they want me to keep an eye on their house, their pets, or their children. I missed the coffee shops and the busy life of being downtown. These thoughts came to me and I opened all the drapes as I love to watch the sky. The air conditioner was running nonstop, and I turned the ceiling fans on, as sleep had finally taken over my body and I had the following dream.

I was walking in a huge courtyard where everything was built out of brick and stone. The huge buildings reminded me of Yale University and underground libraries or a Sunday church where you keep quiet, yet all were in a bigger scale. I saw there was a long walkway and everything looked so peaceful and quiet. There was a fountain in the middle and a huge statue of the Virgin Mary.

I heard voices and saw a group of men talking amongst themselves. They all had very olden day looking clothes on. I wondered where I was that people still dress like this. I started to laugh to myself and said out loud, "I would love to live here like a nun." I am different in this way as I believe in marriage, divorce, love, families, and being modest.

I thought I had moved back to a time zone that I was made to be in, where modesty was still a virtue, not a burden. I started to cry as tears rolled from nowhere. I began to pray to God why was I born in a different era where being celibate is a curse, and not dating is wrong? You are made to feel like something is wrong with you if you want to be just by yourself. I believe divorce is a virtue, not a curse. A marriage made in Hell is the curse you should walk out of with The Lord's blessings.

No one has a right to the mind, body, and soul, but God and only God. I started to repent and asked The Lord to forgive my sins as life places upon our plates the virtues of this world and even though some are not by choice, they still land upon our door. I also believe strongly we the judged should not judge and let basic moral values be our guide. My thoughts kept coming to my mind as I think I was confessing my sins of the mind. My personal belief is you should always confess to yourself and never hold a grudge.

As I was praying silently, I saw a man watching me. I was worried, did I pray out loud? I really thought I was praying in my mind. A gentleman came closer to me as he asked, "May I have a hug?" I am so reserved that I always say no, but I agreed and hugged him.

I said, "Archangel Gabriel," as I knew him from my soul. He hugged me and I asked, "Was I speaking out loud? Did I disturb them? Did you hear me?" He laughed and said, "No, you were not speaking out loud, but yes, I heard you as we can hear even when you say it within your mind." I saw next to him stood Archangel Michael. Now how I knew about their identities, I don't know, although in my dream, I knew them very well.

They sat next to me and told me, "So you heard the news about the Pope?" I told them I am not a Catholic. I am a spiritual person and believe all religions are a highway to Heaven and life is a long highway. The journey of life is a one-way road to Earth called the path to birth. The one-way road to death, is called the path to Heaven. There is also on this one-way road, the bad deed road, which is called wrong way and leads directly to Hell.

The Archangels laughed and hugged me and said, "Throughout this road, we hear you repent for yourself and all around you." I laughed and told them it was my habit for how can the creation but judge another creation? I do, however, repent for the people around me. When I feel like a sin has been committed by someone, without saying anything, I try to repent for them.

They said, "We always hope all the humans repent like you." I cried as we walked for a long time and I asked them, "What is going on? Where am I? And why am I seeing this? I am just an ordinary woman. Why do I see these blessed dreams?" I saw Archangel Gabriel watching over me as he said, "The Pope is resigning and we are trying to see that no evil takes over and everything is okay." I asked, "Why is he resigning? What is wrong?"

I asked, "Did God give him a dream and is this why he is resigning?" The Archangels had said, "He has seen some dreams and for this reason, he thinks it's time he should walk out." I asked, "What? Is he wrong in saying that the Romans had killed the Son of God? Is that not true?" They did not answer, but just walked with me and told me, "Everything is what it is and with faith, everything but is."

I listened to them and told them, "I hear these complicated words of wisdom, but truth be told, I don't understand but just pretend to understand." Again, I got a big hug and they said,

"Remember. Everything begins for now it's time. The change will be." I told them, "I love all religions, but if all religions are true, then who is wrong?"

I was brave and voiced my biggest concern, "Are all religions going to Hell, for every other one says they are going to Heaven and all others are going to Hell. So, my conclusion, are all religions going to Hell?" They asked, "Why do you ask this question?" I told them, "Well, I love all people and everyone says they are right, so how can I go to Heaven and watch others go to Hell? Or how would they go to Heaven and watch others go to Hell? I feel like it is similar to a building catching on fire and one would run to save his or her own life, and not do anything to save the others."

They hugged me again and said, "If there is a person like you crying for all the known and unknown people and faiths of this world, then there shall be peace on Earth and Heaven." The Angels repeated my phrase, "Just follow the basic moral values."

I saw people were talking about something and were worried as I knew something was going on. I knew a lot of changes will take over the world as people have become more and more selfish. I worried why would a Pope resign? I had told The Archangels, "Then, everything shall be fine. The Lord is watching over us always."

I woke up with a fear in my mind and body. What did I see? Why did I see this? Again, I had shared this dream with my friends and we decided to keep a diary and not talk about it as everyone on this Earth has something to say, but no one has any solution to give.

I felt there were too many critics and not enough people praising one another. I kept all my feelings again to myself. I did share with my local church pastor about my holy dreams and to the church, but they all just listened and said these miracles do happen as The Holy Spirit shows us dreams and only The Lord knows why.

I knew a lot of comments will come and too many critics, but I remembered The Archangels repeating "Basic moral values. If only all humans would follow basic moral values, then all would be in peace." My advice for all is please follow the basic moral values. Don't judge one another even if your religious values differ from each other for we all have one Creator, and always we are all on this journey as the creation.

About six months later, on February 11, 2013, Pope Benedict had resigned. Again, I would like all of you to always remember do not become the critic you all dislike when it is you who are being criticized. Let us the human not become The Judge for remember we are all but the judged.

Watching over all of us are The Angels, the guiding lights, The Lord's miracle from beyond our knowledge and time. Forever I know watching over all of us, guiding us back onto the right path is as always from the unknown ocean, the Spiritual Lighthouse.

CHAPTER SEVENTEEN

Spiritual Wagon, The Ferris Wheel Of Reincarnation

"Spiritual wagon travels the same route looking for passengers. She picks up different passengers each time. She cries out, 'Get a second chance with a new ticket and this time, make it to your destination!'"

-Ann Marie Ruby

August 27, 2016

A beautiful summer night in Seattle, Washington. I love the summer as it gifts us long lasting nights. I had fixed up my covered deck with brand new paint and a ceiling fan with flowers carved in as details, a small art design that grabbed my heart, which I love watching. I had planted jasmine flowers in hanging baskets. On the hillside, I had wisteria plants which came back above the deck.

I love sitting on my deck, watching the ferry boats and all the gifts Mother Nature but blesses us with. All my love for Mother Nature blooms every single day as I but enjoy all the gifts she gives us. To top it up, all of this is free of charge. I think it's a mother's pleasure to give without asking for anything in return. I enjoyed this night as she was there watching me just be happy to have her as my companion.

The stars were visible and I thought they were candles glowing throughout the skies. After enjoying all of Mother Nature's gifts to this world, I had decided to turn in as sleep takes over even when sometimes you just want to sit and enjoy the peace and blessings The Lord but has bestowed upon us. As sleep had overtaken my body, my soul had left and traveled to another world. I feel like when we but fall asleep, is it like dying? Or is it like reincarnation? Or is this called an out of body experience?

Dreams have been decoded by experts as all the above and more, for there is no answer to some questions of life. I try to live within the basic rules of the Abrahamic religions as that is how I was brought up to believe. Tonight, upon my door came the question of reincarnation as this is a subject I have tried to avoid.

Life in whole is a miracle where all religions are but on the same highway in pursuit of the truth. Science has supported reincarnation as a possibility. My dream from this night again had awakened me from all personal perception as I believe in reincarnation, for how can I deny what millions of humans but believe?

Within my dream, there again I saw him, a complete stranger yet I knew my soul belonged only to him. I was running and trying to hold on to him. There he was running with me. I had feared the worst as I knew we have only one choice and we must walk up on to the Ferris wheel. We tied a scarf on to our hands to not be separated, and if we were to get separated, then we would have this scarf in between us.

I watched him as we asked each other how is this done? Do we have to just jump off this Ferris wheel and we will end up together again, always forever? I tried to listen, but I knew someone was running after me. I knew I must keep our baby safe. I tried to watch over my husband as he was trying to stay awake and asked me if I would remember everything and if he would remember me. I started to cry as I was lost in my thoughts, for I had no clue. Somehow, I will remember and I will awaken first. Then, I will awaken him after I have but awakened.

The man who was running after me tried to cut us apart. I did not know what happened, but I was crying as I saw my husband jumping down. I had jumped after him from the Ferris wheel and always knew my child was inside my womb. I knew I had landed on my feet and I had to find my husband and my children. All the time, I knew my baby was still within my womb. I walked as one by one, I searched for my family members.

I knew at the end, I had found my husband, but now the only fight was to make him remember our journey from the past. I saw I still had the scarf as I knew he had half of it, but wondered why we were separated and how do we unite. I had no clue about the reality of life. I saw people jumping onto and off the Ferris wheel. I saw on the Ferris wheel, there were children and family members who were separated.

This was a strange dream where all my religious beliefs were being questioned. I knew we have not died and come back to retell what is and what is not, but dreams are lessons from the Heavens above. Where miracles happen, anything is possible. I believe all spiritual miracles do happen at the will of The Omnipotent, for The Omnipotent is the only complete miracle. Spiritual miracles are also called spiritual souls. The belief of twin souls and soulmates is accepted widely within different religious, spiritual, and mythological houses.

The body dies, but the soul lives on as the deeds are counted, and we have Heaven and Hell. It is like reincarnation and our souls live on forever. After my dream, I started to do a lot of research as this was not the first dream on reincarnation I have had, but one of many dreams.

I had to keep an open mind as I believe in miracles all around me happen as days are just passing us by. My dreams have come to life in front of me. I have seen the future, so why would I not see the past? I asked myself this question. The future is given to us through dreams and psychic abilities, but what of the past?

What if the same dreams and psychic abilities can go back in time and talk about the past that are just mysteries? I have had more dreams which came to life in the pages of history as I had Googled my dreams. I have written about these dreams in the other chapters.

In general, I have done a little research on reincarnation dreams and near-death experiences as these are but interlinked within the same mysteries. Doctor Pim van Lommel of the Netherlands has spoken about and done extensive research on hospital based NDEs (near death experiences), a very interesting subject I want all of you to consider and decide for yourself. I will say I believe in miracles.

Doctor Ian Stevenson, former professor of Psychiatry at the University of Virginia, School of Medicine and the former chair of the Department of Psychiatry and Neurology has dedicated a major part of his research to reincarnation. He had indicated to the scientific society with all of his research and scientific evidence that reincarnation just might be true.

I don't know either way what is and what is not, but I will say miracles do happen each and every day of our lives as we see the proof of miracles take place. In this dream, I don't know what was and what was not, but I do believe I have a soulmate who just might be looking for me.

It might have been a way of God letting me know not to give up on anything in life for even when all seem dark and nothing is working out, miracles do happen. For me to be alive and have a blessed life is a miracle. I see and find happiness within the love of a mother and a child, and between the truth and God. Where my Lord is, I am complete with the love of The Omnipotent and The Omnipresence.

Faith is having complete belief in your own way of life. Always within your basket of bread, carry the basic moral values and from there, life takes over her own course. Always keep hope alive and remember even where there is no hope and no way out, there is one, The Omnipotent.

From the dark ocean, The Omnipotent sends all the lost and stranded the eternal light, guiding us back to the truth. I know for all of us within the dark ocean, guiding all the lost and stranded, always standing tall and showing us the light is the Spiritual Lighthouse.

CHAPTER EIGHTEEN

Future Is But The Unknown Phone Number

"Even though the future is not preventable, we the present can give the gift of warnings from the past."

-Ann Marie Ruby

July 22, 2011

I had bought a very nice vacation house in Orlando, Florida. It was a beautiful villa I had loved and wanted to live in forever. My life, however, always plans for herself. I must say though at times, I have felt like my life keeps knocking me off my feet. All my faith I have placed in my Lord and I walk with complete faith.

I know my Lord protects and watches over me at all time. Even when all seem lost, it is what life is all about. Obstacles of life are there as our companions of life. We must learn to live with them and fight every day to overcome all the obstacles, but at all times know this life is a complete blessing from The Lord.

My life journey had me land upon all different corners of life. With complete faith, I traveled this path knowing my Lord is always watching over me. I enjoyed my small villa even though that period, which I call Florida time, was the hardest part of my life. On this day, I had so much going on within my life that I was hardly aware of my surroundings or what was going on around Florida or even the world.

Sometimes, do you too feel like your life is the only thing going on in this universe and everything else is invisible? That was my time and I knew I was being selfish, but I should not worry about myself. Throughout all the struggles and achievements of my life, I never lost my faith and I always had and shall always have within my mind, body, and soul, the love for my Lord.

119

I prayed as I always do when I enter my bed. I feel like each night as we go to bed, our body dies and our soul travels to the unknown zone. This night, I had a very strange dream. I was watching people run and all the people were talking in a language that was foreign to me. I saw children and adults all screaming for help.

I saw a train wreck happening from the sky. It was strange as if I was there, but not there. I asked all to have faith and never lose faith or hope for even though you are in a train wreck, everything shall be alright as tomorrow is another day and even in pain, time heals everything. I cried as I thought what is going on and why is it I am just watching, but not able to help?

I did what I could at that stage. I prayed. I saw all over, there were children, mothers, and fathers trying to help their families. I watched total strangers trying to help each other. My sleep broke as I knew in front of me, I had witnessed a train wreck. I prayed and knew whatever happens, it shall happen for only The Lord can intervene.

This Earthly human could go down on her knees and pray for total strangers. I just wanted to hold, hug, and help even one human if I could. I prayed may all of whom are involved, find the strength to go on. Nothing was in the news, so I had moved on with my life until July 24th.

On July 24, 2011, there really was a train accident in China involving bullet trains. Lightning hit one train, cutting off power. Another train came from behind and hit the train that was stopped in front. This was a shock as I could not believe a dream so vivid and alive had taken place within my dreams in the past and was now being played out in the present.

I prayed to The Lord and wished I could have prevented this. How could I have prevented this, for then what do I say? These thoughts left me as I told myself it's not what I could have done, but I will pray and make sure my Lord gives strength and courage to all of humanity to deal with what is not within our knowledge, but what we must go through. May we also have enough courage and willpower to overcome all the obstacles of life.

Always have faith and try to be there for all of humanity, not only for those of whom but help us, but for those of whom do not ask but are also suffering. May we the humans be there for all humans. Always know for all help and guidance, The Lord has sent to us within the dark ocean, guiding and holding on to all the creation, the Spiritual Lighthouse.

CHAPTER NINETEEN

A Knight's Promise

"History wipes our tears from the past as she guides us into the future with caution and love."

-Ann Marie Ruby

January 10, 2015

A cold winter night. I love the sweet, cold nights. Christmas was over as I had just taken the Christmas tree down. I placed all the decorations away for another year. I always reuse my tree as allergies prevent me from buying a freshly cut tree. I love decorating each year with something new, but reusing most of the same decorations.

I was living in a European style apartment with private courtyards within Downtown Seattle. I loved it here as I had people when I wanted to be with them and the comfort of a quiet courtyard when I just wanted peace. I had Juliet balconies off my bedroom and the living room with a view of the courtyard. The whole city was alive with jingle bells and street decorations from the holidays, all coming down now.

The French bakery next to my apartment was now quiet and coffee was always great at the café downstairs. It was open until 11 PM which was good for a late-night coffee, or if you just wanted to see some people on a break.

I am a person who turns into bed with coffee in my hands. Strange, I am trying to change this habit and have green tea with lemon as a substitute. This night, I had kept my sliding doors closed, but the drapes open to view the mysterious fog outside. The fireplace was on and sometime during the night, I fell asleep as I had the following dream.

I was running through a bridge that was linked to a castle. There was a draw bridge or a stone bridge that led to and from the castle over a moat. I thought this was a very old castle and the land looked like a low-lying area.

I kept looking back at the castle as I was scared and running for my life. I knew I was waiting for my husband to come back as he was not there and had left for work or something. He was missing. I also knew our wedding was held in private, so not all but a few friends knew about our wedding. I was scared and feared what would happen to him.

Where was he? I knew I would die, but never leave him. It was dark and cold as I heard screams had taken over the night skies. There were a lot of women who were wearing chains on their feet and were being held prisoners as they were being called witches. I started to cry as I was worried about my unborn child and what would happen to him. I kept watching a knight who was just standing and watching all of this take place. All the women were being weighed and their fate was being decided.

I knew my huge draped clothing had hidden my child, but I could not tell anyone I was married and pregnant with this child. I started to pray and asked The Lord to protect my child. I knew I would never be accused of being a witch, but I had argued with all the people who were unjustly burning another human being for being different. Some people were making false accusations and just trying to get revenge for personal reasons. I cried as I knew accusing an innocent only takes a false word of accusation, yet undoing this history, will never be.

The dream was really confusing as I don't know what was happening. I saw I had told people I am a healer and I heal with herbs. I know The Lord had given me strength to heal, and all of these women were healers like me. I was saying, "If you trust me, please trust your inner heart. Do not punish an innocent for being different. If someone does wrong, do punish them, but if someone can heal and help you recover from your fever, how could you after being healed go and call them witches?"

I warned all to be aware of The Lord, "Know all that you are doing will come back and haunt you through history." I watched so many women were being taken to prison and so much injustice was being carried out. Women were being raped and thrown out like trash. They were being thrown into a river or a lake or a moat and being drowned. Land after land, throughout different nations, this was going on. I wondered when would this injustice be heard by the hearts of the humans.

I saw there were so many people crying and smells of flesh burning filled the air. I knew my husband was running, and trying to come back and help me as I saw he was white and my skin color was brown like Egyptian or something. He kept screaming to me to hold on and not let go of life. I knew injustice was being done as even the Heavens above were crying. I saw The Archangels standing and watching me as all of this was happening in front of me. I cried and told The Holy Angels I can't run away and save my life as I see all of these people are being harmed.

I saw there was a man standing and watching me as I met him eye to eye and asked him, "Why are you supporting this as you too have three daughters? Are you not afraid they will grow up to hate you?" I saw he was crying, yet he was too frightened to say anything to his wife who had supported the wrongdoings. I wondered how a woman could kill other innocent women and still live with this. I watched my house and knew all of this was now burned down to ashes as injustice had been done.

I started praying and called upon The Archangels to intervene. I asked, "What is going on? Why are The Angels of Heaven not intervening?" I saw within my hands, I also had a medicine bag which had miraculous cures. I had told a man, "Take this to the house of the Virgin Mary and leave it there in the well. God knows everything and in that house, all shall be safe."

I had to walk for miles to reach a safe place for my baby to be born. I knew I had very little time as I then saw I was going through the river of life. I saw in front of me was the river of life and all the pain would be gone. I knew in between life and death was this river and as soon as the soul reaches this water, life moves on. I wanted my child to be safe and I prayed to God to let my child live.

I saw within this moat, I gave birth to my son. I screamed and cried for my husband, never did I want to leave him. Sometimes life takes you away, with or without one's will. As my son was born, he started to cry. I saw there came the knight who was standing and

126

watching all the wrongdoings take place. He screamed and said to give him my son as he will keep my son safe. I dropped my son within his arms secretly as he jumped into the moat. I knew he would swim away and take my son to safety. As I floated out of my body, I knew life had left my body.

I saw somehow the knight went deep under the water and he came out from somewhere as he was running with my baby. I saw my husband had come back to find out he had lost the love of his life and his son. He screamed and cried and asked the King to stop this unjust burning of the witches and all of whom but support the witches. It was as if you could call someone a witch if you didn't like the person, and have her burned to ashes.

He screamed and fought to have this injustice reversed. He prayed and I watched him search for me all his life. My dream changed as now I saw the same knight was older and walking in a fisherman's village as he was worried about the women who had been burned to ashes. The knight had run away to another country as he crossed the border. He had kept on going until he knew he was safe and the child would be fine within the land.

He had brought up the child as his own and knew from this child will come the future generations of a mother and a father who had fought for justice until their last breath. He had walked and run all the way to a fisherman's village. The knight said this baby will grow up in Rotterdam. What happened to the medicine bag, I have no clue as I knew one day, all humans will look for this medicine bag.

This dream took place after the period of Christ, as the house of the Virgin Mary was known to my soul as a sacred place to be in. This meant I was an early Christian trying to save the witches from being persecuted by other early Christians. All night, I heard The Lord would resurrect and bring back people as the End of Time but approaches.

As my sleep broke, I cried for a long time for I never gave reincarnation a thought in my life as my faith did not allow me. I researched a lot on reincarnation and dreams. I found out even though a lot of religions don't believe in reincarnation, it existed in all the early religions such as early Judaism and early Christianity. Now science too has various research on reincarnation. Edgar Cayce had done extensive research and proved it in his ways.

After so many studies, even science is not ready to say reincarnation does not exist for there is too much evidence proving too many people are having experiences of reincarnation. Science cannot disprove reincarnation as evidence from so many testimonies from people of all different faiths are but rising.

I had walked back in history to see why I had this dream. I found out there were a lot of witch persecutions throughout history. Within Europe, the United States, and all over this world, people were executed even without evidence ever linking them to be a witch.

Throughout Europe, estimates vary greatly listing thousands to millions of people being executed for witchcraft. This European hysteria also caused panic within the United States. False and baseless accusations along with scapegoating had caused executions to many innocent lives in Salem, Massachusetts where over 200 were accused with 20 people and 2 dogs being executed.

This was a dark time when anyone who had any knowledge with any healing powers was burned to ashes or executed using another method. I must say a lot of witches may have done harm to innocent people with their powers. A crime is a crime, and who does it, matters not. I wondered why would people be burned without any justice and how was this normal? If someone has done something wrong, then let the laws of the land be their judge. If an innocent, however, is being punished for being different, then do know The Final Judge, The Omnipotent shall judge you for being The Judge.

I did research about the castle, the knight, and the witches. This is what I found out. There is a weighing house in Oudewater in the Netherlands where witches were weighed. Unlike other cities, people could come here for a fairer trial and get a certificate saying they were not witches as their weight was not significantly lighter than it should be. There were other places in the Netherlands, however, where women thought to be witches were burned or drowned.

There really is a fisherman's village in Rotterdam in the Netherlands, as I saw in my dream. So, I believe the honorable knight was a witness to so much injustice. He did save my son and had brought him to the Netherlands to be within the safety of this mystical land. It is said that the castles throughout Europe are still haunted. I wonder what is haunting these castles, witches for being different or being bad? Or the people who have judged them for being different? I live in a time zone in which I know we would love to be different, but I see what being different has done to even an open society like mine.

What does my dream have anything to do with the history of these stories? I don't know. I don't know what had happened in the past. I woke up missing a husband and a child I don't know about. I had taken this night as a movie from the past which even throughout time, is alive, buried within the memories of the past.

Maybe one day, I will have all the answers or some of the answers to my dream. I, however, prayed for the Netherlands where so many innocent lives were saved because of the weighing house for I know a good deed is always rewarded throughout time. When all of this misery was going on all over Europe, many had the chance of escaping to Oudewater, in hope of getting a fairer trial. The weighing scales to measure the witches still exist in the Netherlands. I had not yet been to the Netherlands when I had seen this dream.

After finishing my dream diaries, I had taken a short trip to this faraway land. I know history, even though not so nice at times, is out there as a teacher of life. History comes upon our door in the present as whispers from the past, sometimes singing sweet, loving songs and in this one case, the tune was tragic and of sorrow. Sometimes, it takes a tragedy to teach us the humans.

This story from the past, proven or not, has taught all of us in the future to accept all different people into one nation. In the United States, we live as one nation under God, and in the

Netherlands, they have one of the most tolerant cultures worldwide with a beautiful country. The Netherlands is a peaceful country, which I know from my dream and research afterwards.

Message from this dream is do not disbelieve in the miracles of the past, present, or the future, as the beautiful windmills of the Netherlands, the tulip grounds, and the lighthouses all over the country sing the tunes of hope and union all over the lands. Keep the rays of hope alive within your soul, for throughout the universe from within the dark oceans, always guiding all throughout eternity is the Spiritual Lighthouse.

CHAPTER TWENTY

Bridge Of Mercy

"Embark upon this journey of life with mercy as your guide. Be merciful to all wondering eyes, for is not what you search for within all, but Mercy?"

-Ann Marie Ruby

October 8, 2016

Cool October night in greater Seattle, Washington area. The Puget Sound and the Olympic Mountains form a beautiful and scenic frame around my house. Nature is my spiritual inspiration in daily life. I enjoyed the cool, quiet, and peaceful night all by myself with a good book.

My bedroom windows frame the Puget Sound and the Olympic Mountains as I keep no drapes but always fall asleep to this peaceful and serene nature. I give grace to my Lord for all of what The Lord has blessed me with. I have had a very hard life and I always try to find the best in even the worst of things. Life is a blessing as we have this day as a glimpse of hope sparkling in the sky.

I know always after the dark night's sky, dawn breaks open pouring down all of her glory. If tonight, you are going to bed with tears rolling from your eyes, physically or emotionally drained out in pain, remember The Lord brings dawn back after the dark night's sky. Tomorrow always shines within our reach. I prayed for a long time this night as I knew someone, somewhere out there, was sleeping with a heavy heart. May my prayers reach your doors all my friends. When they come knocking on your doors, please accept them, and open the door as you accept the prayer as a gift from a friend.

Sleep came within my tired mind and body as I had a very strange dream this night. I did have my doubt if this dream would

133

make it to the pages of my dream diaries. I decided to share this dream, thinking maybe someone out there needs this message from the Heavens above.

I saw a man sitting on a chair watching the windows which had views of a river flowing through a valley. There was a bridge connecting two valleys. On one side of the bridge, there stood smiling the Virgin Mary. She was wearing a white and blue gown and had her hands in a prayer position. On the other side of the bridge, was a huge light and there I knew standing tall was The Holy Spirit. The light shining from The Holy Spirit to the Virgin Mary was very peaceful and I knew this was the most blessed bridge of all existence. In my dream, I kept on calling this bridge, "The Bridge of Mercy."

I was now inside the apartment of this man watching this beautiful bridge. I saw I was with The Holy Archangel Gabriel and Archangel Michael. I asked them, "What is going on? Where am I? And who is this man?" The Archangels had told me the name of the person who I knew was a homosexual man.

He was stuck inside this room, but somehow, he remembered his mother. I watched his eyes tear up. He was crying as he was traveling through memory lanes. He knew something bad had happened. He remembered his father and cried for a long time. His mother was an artist or was an honorable person, who had painted this beautiful painting. He had this painting in his hands. As he placed the painting on an easel, tears drowned him in the ocean of sadness.

I asked him why he was crying as he saw me and he said he is a sinner and he does not know how to be in the mercy of The Lord if he had gone against The Lord and The Lord's will. He showed me the painting as it was so beautiful and represented mercy. The glow of The Holy Spirit entered the room as I watched the man. I asked The Holy Spirit, "Is there no hope for this man? Why has he broken down like this?" The Holy Spirit replied, "There is always hope for all."

I heard The Holy Archangel Michael ask me, "Do you remember the prayer you had written?" I said, "Yes I do. 'Blessings Of The Mercy.'" I kissed the man's head and told him, "I am like a sister to you. May I have a hug?" We hugged and I told him, "Remember, there is always hope for all of the humans for we are but the judged and The Final Judge is the one we all answer to. There is hope for all of us for I don't know my own sins or yours. Only God is The Judge. But for all, we have the blessed prayers."

I said, "The prayer 'Forgiveness, Redemption, And Awakening.'" I also had recited, "The difference between the sinner and the pious is the Door of Repentance."

I heard The Angels repeat, "He is a good soul. May the message spread that no one is to judge but The Omnipotent." They repeated, "Pure love of The Omnipotent is so much more than all sin or sinners combined." I saw the person had given me the painting as a gift which read *Mercy*.

I had awakened in the middle of the night as I cried for all different race, color, and religion. I looked up "Mercy" on the internet on my phone and found out that Pope Francis had announced this year to be the Year of Mercy. My phone had notified me today all different religions all over the world were celebrating different holy occasions. I prayed to The Lord, "May the Bridge of Mercy be upon all humans and may we all repent, redeem, and be awakened."

I thought about the person I had seen in my dream, and I knew I saw him as a person who had passed away. I thought he had died, but his soul was not in peace. Within my dream, I had hugged this person and called him my brother as I said I will pray for his soul and may he find peace. I don't know who he was, but know I will in my lifetime be in touch with his family members somehow.

I thought if only all the humans had carried within their souls the power of repentance. I tried to do some research and found that Pope Francis had said the power of repentance overweighed the sins. I saw in Hinduism, in Christianity, in the basics of all religions, they talk about sins and repentance. I was so happy knowing all we have to do when we know we have but sinned is repent, redeem, and awaken, and not repeat the sin. I guess in my mind, this formula was easy as in worldly terms we would say even on Earth, repeated offenders don't get another chance.

The Lord is so merciful. May The Lord's blessings be upon all humans for all we have to do is repent. I thought about the people who have but passed away without repenting. What about them? So, I ask you the family members and the friends of the deceased, please repent for yourself first and then for all of your family members whom have passed away. It is like how you put your seatbelt on first, then your child's seatbelt. Repent for all even if they have repented or not, do repent.

I prayed for the unknown person as I know even though life did not give us a chance to meet, I know I will meet his family members and may they know this sister will always pray for all of you as I repent first and pray afterwards for all. I had awakened to a prayer which I was reciting within my dreams.

BLESSINGS OF THE MERCY[3]

Oh my Lord,

Today give us but the Gift of Mercy.

For on this day,

I ask of You for mercy.

Where all but is lost,

Where nothing is but found,

Where hearts are but broken

Where nothing but sorrow engulfs,

I ask You, My Lord, for mercy.

My Lord, my Creator,

Let The Bridge of Mercy but appear.

My Lord, let The Bridge of Hope

[3] From my previous book of spiritual prayers, *Spiritual Songs: Letters From My Chest*

But shine up in the dark, lost ocean.

My Lord, let this sinner be not lost.

My Lord, may my heart find You

And may this be my awakening.

My Lord, My Creator,

May my heart beat only for You

As I walk upon this bridge.

For I know even when all is but lost,

All is but dark,

And all but is fading away,

It is then I find the mercy of my Lord,

In the dark, in the light, always waiting for me.

It was I who but did not see You, my Lord.

It was I who but was lost my Lord.

It was I who but got onto

The wrong boats my Lord.

My Lord, My Creator,

Without a word, a sound, or giving us a glimpse, Walks silently,

gracefully,

With hands shining like the stars,

Feet glowing like the moon,

My Lord walks and leaves upon us,

The

BLESSINGS OF THE

MERCY

May this prayer be within your mind, body, and soul as it comes from my soul. May all of us know even through the dark nights and when the days seem even darker, always watching over all of the lost and stranded souls from the deep dark ocean, is the Spiritual Lighthouse.

CHAPTER TWENTY-ONE

Faith Is Believing, Not Questioning

"A new beginning is but not the end. Know the truth as all but end, it is then all but begin again."

-Ann Marie Ruby

May 26, 2013

I was living in Arizona after I had bought my dream ranch house. Surrounded by mountains in the middle of the desert in a quiet golf community, I had found my dream house. I had renovated the house and knew this is a one of a kind home, not for everyone but I loved it. Five acres of land with bull snakes, rattlesnakes, coyotes, cute bunnies and rabbits hopping and eating all the vegetables, and birds singing sweet love songs as Mother Nature gives all of this in a package deal as a gift to the beholders.

I had to use a walking stick when I walked my puppy as no one wants to run into a rattlesnake. The best part was every night after sunset, my neighbor's cows would walk over to my land somehow over the fence or they might have had a private route through which they came over. I loved the sounds of the cows and roosters every morning. I loved the heated days and the cold mornings with the morning fog.

Life though has her own ways and as life had it, I had to move, but this time with a lot of tears and pain as I loved this quiet space and if I could, I would have stayed here for the rest of my life. I had no clue as to what I should do with the house as I just wanted to lock the doors and keep her waiting for me as I would retire and come back home to her.

I decided that's what I would do. I would just keep the house, and rent when I reached my destination. I had seen a blessed dream

141

that night as I had gone to sleep after I prayed for a long time for guidance.

I saw there was a lot of people in my house. A gentleman had been showing my house around to strangers. I knew I had bought the house cash, so I really did not need to sell. On top of it, I really loved the house, and had thought it to be my retirement property. I talked with the man walking all around my house.
I asked him, "Who are you? What is going on?" I saw there was a light shining all over him and I felt comfortable talking with him.

I told him all about my life and cried for a long time as I thought I was talking with an Angel. He said nothing, but hugged me and then said, "Have faith always, for God is always watching over." I told him, "I feel like my life is filled with obstacles after obstacles."

Sometimes you would think if you are trying to follow the Commandments of The Lord, people and family would leave you alone. It's not like I am an Angel. I have sinned and I repent every day for known and unknown sins. I just don't know what to do. This was a place far away from all the glitters of life, and I thought I could have a quiet and peaceful life here.

He laughed and asked me, "But what if The Lord has another plan for you?" I told him, "I just wrote a prayer, 'For You, My Lord, I But Am.'" He asked, "Have you finished your prayer book?" I told him, "Not yet." He asked me, "Do you know who I am?" I told him, "Yes, I do. You are Archangel Gabriel. I always see Archangel Michael asking me to write the prayer book."

He said then, "Nice to meet you. I am Gabriel, Archangel Gabriel." I told him, "It's so nice to see you, but I know this is only a dream and as my dream breaks, I will still be stuck with all the troubles of life."

I knew I am all alone and have to deal with all of these obstacles by myself. I had broken down in tears as I told him, "It is the religious belief that has taken me far away from my family and my church. I believe all religion, race, and color should have the same respect. Humans should be valued with their basic moral values. I don't like walking into a church or any religious worshiping house to be told that all other humans will go to Hell, but one group of people."

I asked Archangel Gabriel, "If Christians call out on each other, condemning each other, then what about all the different groups of religions?" He hugged me and said, "There is only one Creator and all creation are but The Lord's creation. They can condemn each other, but do they not think, what if The Lord had condemned these acts?"

I told him, "I think about how we the adults teach the children to be kind and nice to all. But, what happens to these houses of worshipping? How can they judge each other? I will write my prayer book for all race, color, and religion. I have written a prayer called, 'May We The Judged Not Be The Judge.'"

I spoke with him for a long time as he told me, "God loves all the creation equally. It is the creation who but separate from each other by sins." I saw as we were walking, morning was approaching

143

and I asked him, "What should I do about my house? I love living here, but I don't know what to do or how to move on with my life." He said, "Watch."

As I followed his gaze, I saw a man walking on top of my roof with a "For Sale" sign in his hands. Then, I watched him place the "Sold" sign on top of the house.

He then jumped down from the roof and said, "May I have a hug?" I hugged him as he introduced himself as Archangel Michael. I watched both and thought even if you two don't show up in my awakening stage, I will follow your advice forever. I know faith is believing, not questioning, so I will follow only my Lord's will. I had also followed common sense. Could I move? Should I move?

This night, I had a simple answer to a complicated situation I had faced within my life. I had prayed for guidance as to which path I should go on at that time of my life. The Lord had answered my prayers within my dreams. I woke up and had placed my house on the market with an agent named Michael. I had told him about my dream as the agent had said the first time he walked in, "May I have a hug?" He told me he has seen and met so many people, but somehow, he felt at peace when he walked into my house.

After a few days, Michael had called me and told me he had felt like praying as he had walked into my house to show the house to a couple. He said he had an offer on the spot and he will take care of all the details. The house had sold. It was not a very hard decision to make as I always follow my Lord's messages from beyond. I believe the house was not the right choice for a young and single woman like me in a remote place in the dessert. I know sometimes we are hurt at the setbacks and all the negative aspects of life, the hurdles, or my personal favorite phrase, obstacles of life. I also believe obstacles are teachers of life, and as we have crossed them, we have learned our lessons.

This is my advice for all of you whom are confused about religion, life, or just the obstacles of life. Believe in yourself and know how and whatever name you might call your Creator by, it is okay, for The Omnipotent is there watching over us. The Lord knows what humans, saints, or any religious gurus don't know. The Lord is merciful. This dream I have included for within this dream, I realized, do call upon The Creator for guidance as whatever the troubles are, there is a simple solution which I call "prayer."

Always remember, it matters not how hard life is and where life but places us, we will survive. For always from the skies up in the Heavens, The Lord watches over all without judging or condemning our actions of life, if we live within the Commandments and with basic moral values. I also believe the best partner for life is repentance from the soul as I say each and every day, "I repent, redeem, and awaken for my Lord." From the unknown, unseen ocean of life, always watching over all of us out there is the Spiritual Lighthouse.

CHAPTER TWENTY-TWO

Bridge Between All Cultures Is But Love

"Be the spiritual traveler who journeys through different race, color, and religion to create the bridge of union."

-Ann Marie Ruby

March 21, 2013

Living in Arizona was an amazing gift for my life. Arizona was a very friendly state with so much to offer for all different race, color, and religion. I have lived in different states within the United States throughout my life and have had the fortune to travel overseas and live in different parts of this world. Life is a miracle and having all different race, color, and religion is a gift from The Creator. I believe for some reason unknown to us the humans, The Lord has created these cultures.

It is for The Lord's knowledge and The Lord's will that all of us live on this Earth. Not always in union, but we share the same Mother Earth, living under the same skies. How do we live and share the same water, the same air, heat, Earth, and space without getting to know each other or being friendly toward each other? I had a very strange dream this night as I had no clue for I was ignorant about different cultures even after traveling around the world.

I was walking in a hilly area as I could see the houses across the hills and around the hills. It was an amazing place and very calm and pleasing to the soul. I saw there was water running across the land like a lake and people were fishing. I saw the people were living life in peace and harmony. I realized I walked into Native American territory.

An elderly man came out of his stucco house and asked me to come and sit with him. I sat there and knew he was one of two brothers who ruled the small village and his tribe called him

147

respectfully, a leader of their tribe. He asked me, "You have been traveling for so long and finally you have come to meet me." I told him, "I did not know you were expecting my visit," He said, "I have been waiting for you. How are you doing?"

I told him I had brought corn, bread, and potatoes for him as I was a vegetarian, but I have brought enough for his tribe. I remember giving him a lot of corn, bread, and potatoes for all to share. I spoke with the gentleman for a long time as I explained The Holy Spirit works in miracles and even though we the humans confuse all the religions, The Lord knows the truth. I told him there is only one Omnipotent and all the rest is just we the creation dividing amongst each other.

I told him if only we could all be equal and not be greater or lesser than each other. If we could all hold on to the blessed word "love" for then there would be no war amongst the humans. I walked all over the place and somehow talked about a river or a lake where people go for fishing. I loved how even to this day, people are trying to save the heritage of their families.

I saw as time passed by, within their groups, they also had crime, violence, and sickness as these have entered throughout the world. The elderly man had spoken about The Great Spirit as I only listened to him. I knew sometimes, you just have to be the ears and let the other speak. How would I be fair if I only talked about my life and not about theirs? There was a beautiful rainbow in the skies as we were walking and I held his very old and wise hands, and hugged him.

148

My dream broke, but I knew I would see this kind gentleman sometime in the future and it would be so nice to see a kind-hearted soul. I woke up and decided to go for a visit to the Navajo Nation. I had loved going there and had met a nice tourist advisor. I found out that they believe a woman had brought corn and bread to their lands.

I was shocked as in my dream, I had taken corn and bread to the nice gentleman which he had shared with all the land. I also met a lot of friendly people who had gone to a bazaar to sell blankets and handmade goods. There was a family sitting in the corner and amongst them, I saw a woman sitting with tears in her eyes. I know these days, you mind your own business and stay away from all other people. You don't place your nose in anyone's business. I thought well, no one here knows me and if they hate me, I will leave as soon as I get in my car, but I must give that woman a hug before I go. I walked over and asked her if she was okay and if she needed help. She told me her story.

She was married to the love of her life just for a week. As she had found out her husband was dying from cancer, she married him with the knowledge that their love story would be very short-lived. She told me it was worth it, even if that meant she would have him only for a day. I cried with her as her in-laws were all siting with her now.

They were selling blankets in the bazaar and thought she needed to be out with people as they had just buried their son a few days ago. She was a wife for a week and she was still wearing her wedding ring. I hugged her and told her to know she had him forever, as even a day is worth all of the years of life. Love lives on and I asked her to find him within the love of humanity. Whenever and wherever there is love, try to find him. We had spoken for a long time, and even though we were of different race, color, and religion, we shared the same tears of love.

I told them I just wrote a prayer and if they did not mind, we could all recite together. I am not like this, as I am a very private person and never do I just go out and talk with strangers. They were so happy as we held hands and in a circle, we recited a prayer I had just written that very day.

LIFE ON THIS EARTH IS BUT A DAY[4]

My Lord The Most Merciful,
I seek forgiveness in You from all sins of this day.
May my day be filled with Your mercy.
May I be only on Your Path throughout my day.
May I be an example of Your true devotee.
May my prayers reach Your Door my Lord.
May the mornings be glorified
With Your blessings my Lord.
May the sun shine throughout every household
On this Earth in Your name my Lord.

[4] From my previous book of spiritual prayers, *Spiritual Songs: Letters From My Chest*

150

May all Your creation know of their Lord,

The Omnipotent, before night falls my Lord.

May all of Your children know my Lord,

LIFE ON THIS EARTH IS
BUT A DAY.

I came home that night very tired and felt a strange relief. Why would I write this prayer and why would I meet this family? They had taken this prayer with them as she said she felt God had sent her a message through me to let her know life is but a day and live it gracefully to the best as you can.

Always know The Lord is there watching over all of us. She also believed in resurrection and all loved ones shall unite when it is but time. The corn and bread also was a thought that came to my mind. I knew I had seen so many people, but I don't believe I had seen my friend from my dream as I remembered he had said finally we meet.

I don't know when we will meet, but I know he was like a grandfather I would love to have and hug. Until we do meet, I keep this dream in my heart alive. The message for all of you is take my prayer as a gift and know, whatever is going on in your life and if the struggles seem like a mountain, just hold on to the prayers of life and life shall be a blessing as my newly found friend went home in peace as she said forever in her life she will recite this prayer each and every day.

For all of you my friends, remember even when all are lost and all seem stranded, out there guiding us from the beyond is always, the Spiritual Lighthouse.

CHAPTER TWENTY-THREE

Repentance, The Bridge To Heaven

"Forgiveness comes from the core of humanity. Without the core, the apple is but nothing. Without forgiveness, humans are but extinct."

-Ann Marie Ruby

January 29, 2014

Seattle, Washington where all race, color, and religion mingle on the same road. Humans carry within themselves humanity. Every day, the roads are but witnesses to so many tales of history. If only the roads could talk. Today, a friend came over as she was walking home from the Downtown Macy's store. Life had changed for her today. When she was on the phone with me earlier, I heard a big scream and my life had stopped in fear.

What had just happened? She was screaming and I heard people screaming. I thought the world had ended for all involved in the incident. I was in the dark as I could only hear what was going on at the other end, but not see anything. My friend spoke after a while as she just witnessed an accident. A man was trying to cross at the cross section when he had the right of way.

A car just came from nowhere and ran over him, in the middle of a busy road. She said all the passerby people stopped over and started to hold hand in hand as all created a bridge of human bodies so no car could go over the man who was now bleeding in the middle of the road. There were doctors and nurses tending to him. As the ambulance had come, he was talking and everyone, all race, color, and religion started to pray for him.

He thanked all the unknown people as he was taken into the ambulance. Other unknown people went with him in the ambulance holding on to his personal belongings until his family members could arrive.

The man lived today for all the kind-hearted people we but think don't exist anymore. I call these people Angels in disguise. This night, I had prayed for all race, color, and religion to find peace within the bond of love amongst all humans. Sleep came over as I had the following dream.

I was walking in the middle of a place, but I could not figure out where I was. I wondered, where was I? I saw all around there was death, and the horror of death filled the air. I saw the dead were being carried to the churches and some to worshipping places of other religions and faiths to be buried. I knew all around were people of different faiths and I was worried what happens after death.

I saw now, there was a man who was being taken by The Angels as he had passed away. I saw he was tagged a sinner and for his sins, he was being taken to Hell directly. I saw the man was a complete stranger, yet I could feel his complete feelings. I could feel his fear and his terror as I started to cry for him.

I started to cry to The Holy Spirit as I bent over and started to pray. I saw in front of me were The Holy Archangels of Heaven. They said, "Watch." I saw the man was crying as he was a sinner and all throughout his life, he had lived within sin. He was born in an orphanage and never knew what to do about religion. He never followed one religion as all the different religions confused him. He knew he had no basic moral values as he always blamed everything all around him for all things that had gone wrong within his life and for being an orphan.

He had blamed God for not giving him a family or anyone to guide him. So, he never tried to fix anything, but kept a grudge over life. At the end of his life, he wanted to follow a religion or a faith, but did not know which house to enter and how to pray. He had bought a prayer book he had found on the internet for all race, color, and religion. He had recited a prayer within the book that was written by someone who said even if all is but lost, repent.

He was reciting the repentance prayer and had called The Omnipotent to accept his repentance and punish him for his sins. He asked The Omnipotent to accept him as he too is a creation who belonged within no house of faith, yet he is a creation of The One Creator, The Omnipotent. He cried to The Omnipotent and asked what is his sin. He only knew what was taught to him. Every one of the existing religions claim they belong in Heaven and all others belong in Hell. So, do all people then go to Hell?

The Archangels had heard him and within his dreams, they had come to visit him. They had told him The Lord accepts the repentance from the soul. The Creator has given all humans on Earth the biggest grace through repentance. When repentance comes from the soul, The Lord but hears. They told him if he has no religion to follow or any guidelines to live by, then follow basic moral values. They coincide with all different religions and messages.

I saw on his chest was a book which had written on it, *Spiritual Songs*. Archangel Michael then asked me, "Have you written the songs yet?"

I asked him, "What? I am confused for as a Christian, we are taught to repent and let all faiths coincide with each other. All religions teach the same message. Why don't we realize and just pray even in normal worldly terms?" Then, Archangel Gabriel had asked, "The songs, have you written them yet?"

I told them I want to write a prayer book for all race, color, and religion, something we the creation could recite even without any religious background, just from each soul to The Creator. I told them my only fear is what about all the critics? What will they say? I don't ever want to be known or criticized. I just want to live my life in peace.

They watched me and said they understood this world is hard, but also within this world, there are some people who need a sister, or a brother to hold their hands even outside of a religious house and say with the purest heart, "Just repent to your Creator from your house." I did say to The Archangels, "Would this not be called a contradiction of faith?"

I then realized no. It would not be a contradiction for if I had something all race, color, and religion could recite in union and individually that had no religious background, but for all creation of The Creator, then it would just be a book.

The Angels had hugged me and said, "Anyone is welcome in the House of The Lord for all are but the creation. No human can stop another human from entering the Doors of Heaven." I asked them, "So, how do we enter Heaven?" They replied, "Repentance, the Bridge to Heaven."

I awoke with a very heavy heart as because of my Earthly fear, I had not published my prayer book. It is so strange I was not afraid of my Lord, but was concerned about humans and what they would say and not say. I thought why did humans have so much power over even God? I knew not a single human could help one another go to Heaven. Everyone must enter Heaven with his or her own life diaries.

As the sun streamed in through the night's sky, I thought would all these voices that are so powerful and strong help on the final Judgment Day? What would they say? I knew I had to do something for myself, for my love of all humans. For those of you whom don't have any house of worship to go to, for all of you, I have written my songs, a prayer book for all race, color, and religion.

This book is not in any way affiliated with any religion, yet it respects all religions and whatever you call your Lord, I call my Lord, The Omnipotent. You can call The Lord by any name, but there is only one Creator. Repent with your own words like, "My Lord, forgive this Earthly sinner. Accept my repentance." Repent from your soul and follow the basic moral values.

Message for all of you whom need a helping hand to find yourself, know it's you who must speak up and not get drained away in the loud voices of the strangers whom but only make sounds. When you must talk and stand up, no one will be there to help you for remember even though they might seem powerful and very noisy, on that day, all must talk and walk on their own on that road.

So, I ask you all to seek, ask, and knock within your souls and know there is no difference in how and where you call upon The Omnipotent. There awaits upon the Heavens, The Omnipotent, The Omnipresence, The Alpha, The Omega, The Creator of all creation. I ask all of you not to lose yourself within the lost and stranded, for always remember from the dark oceans, guiding all lost and stranded souls is always, the Spiritual Lighthouse.

CHAPTER TWENTY-FOUR

The Ark Of Humanity

"Basic moral values carry all humans upon the Ark of humanity."

-Ann Marie Ruby

September 26, 2011

Orlando, Florida, vacation land, tourist destination, for me was to be my vacation home, where I would eventually retire. I was so happy I had finally made it. I had a nice vacation villa where life could be simple and easy. Preplanning for retirement at an early age was a dream come true. Life on the other hand has her own ways. Life takes us on a roller coaster her own way.

Preplanning is always a good idea, but do not be disappointed if life gives you everything and then takes all away. I have found peace within my sacred love for my Creator, and all the blessings that but come from this pure union. This sacred bond kept me going through all the obstacles of life. At all times, I know I love my Lord more than all the obstacles that can be poured down onto me.

Orlando, Florida was an amazing place to live for the period I had lived there. Life is a blessing and always I believe, obstacles of life are but teachers of life. I learn and walk again. As always, I know The Lord is but always watching over us.

This was a very busy night as I had a lot of work done in the house and visited the theme parks with out of town guests. I came home and fell asleep as soon as I touched my pillow. I am a person who can fall asleep even on the couch if I am sleepy. I can also stay awake without any coffee if I must. Sleep came over as I had the following dream.

I saw there was a ferry boat waiting by the shore. It was a small ferry boat, but as people went aboard the boat, it became larger to fit all of whom were walking onto it. From the outside, however, the boat still looked small.

I heard the captain calling out to all of whom could hear him to get on board the boat. I was trying to help all of the people whom were trying to get onto the boat. I asked the captain, "What is going on? Why do I feel like people must get on the boat? Why am I so worried about all the people who miss the boat? Why is this bothering me?" It's a boat and people can choose if they want to get on the boat or not. Yet, I screamed out to all, begging all to just take another look and come onto the boat.

I knew a storm was coming and somehow, I felt all the people would be safe within this boat, not within the lands, even though general sense would say avoid sea traveling during any storms. I cried and kept saying, "But within this storm, you must take shelter within this boat."

I saw the captain smiling as I thought he just showered and looked so clean and fresh. He had no worries in the world. I watched him as he looked at me directly. I hugged him and said, "Jesus Christ, the son!" I repeated, "Christ the son has come with his boat!" The Ark for all to get aboard was here. I was so happy and then I felt so sad for all of the people whom were so busy with life that they had no time for God or anyone.

Life was complete with each individual and his or her own way of life. I started to cry as I held my hands up in prayer and knelt on my knees as I prayed. I began to talk to my Creator. Life will end for all humans as we are mortal, but then why do we not repent, redeem, and awaken? Why do we not realize and just do it now, and know within each soul, we will not lose anything, but gain spirituality from within our souls.

I watched all the members of the Ark were so calm as they said, "All of whom repent, redeem, and awaken shall be upon this Ark. That is the ticket to this Ark." I repeated, "As simple as that, repenting from the mind, body, and soul."

I watched the captain of the boat stand up as he watched the humans for a long time and said, "That's it. This Ark will leave shore and those of whom have entered are blessed and all the rest are but lost."

I knew they were lost because they were lost within themselves. I prayed not to call upon The Lord just as you need The Lord, but always as The Lord too awaits your call.

I watched the Ark take off and knew that's it. There is nothing I can do to help anyone, so I just dropped my tears and my pillows were drenched wet as my sleep broke.

I wanted to do something more than what I was doing and this thought engulfed me for another five years as I had no clue what can I, a spiritual woman, do for anyone or those of whom don't even believe in eternity.

I had follow up dreams in which I had seen The Holy Archangels asking me to write my prayer book. I finally had the courage to write about my blessed dreams from which I have the dream diaries. For all of you whom are searching for words to recite a prayer, I have for you my prayer book.

I know it is hard for me to ask anyone or tell anyone how to live their lives or their ways of life. This is a subject all differ and have complications to even talk about. I have crossed the bridge of fear in which I was always thinking what will the next person standing next to me think. I have for the first time in my life taken the decision to stand up and write my dreams and my prayers for all of whom ask for them.

I don't want to give power to those who don't need them and block the path for those whom but accept them as a friend. For this reason, I have learned it may take years sometimes, but it is better late than never.

For all of you whom are but seeking the right path, know it's within your soul. I believe there is no difference in any religion and any path you want to follow, it is the right path, if your path has been created with basic moral values.

For all, I have a blessing to give through my prayers which come from no religious background, but basic moral values. I believe if you are lost within the thoughts or confused within the doors of religion, remember always from the ocean of the unknown, guiding us all, invisible to some yet very visible to the believers, is the captain and the Spiritual Lighthouse.

CHAPTER TWENTY-FIVE

Time Travel Through Spiritual Awakening

"Time is but a sacred spiritual journey acquired by the time traveler through sacred spiritual awakening."

-Ann Marie Ruby

May 8, 2012

Arizona, the mountains, the desert, and the beautiful lake complete the perfect picture for this lonely sacred soul. I loved living in the desert with a cottage ranch house on five acres of land. For neighbors, I had cows, goats, and chickens. I had to be careful of the coyotes and rattlesnakes. I always walked with a flashlight as my dog had to go out for his bathroom calls at night.

I kept all the windows open throughout the night as this would keep the entire house cool throughout the day. I don't like running the air conditioner as I love the mountain air. Most houses, however, do have air conditioners although a lot of houses have gone solar.

The windows were blowing in mountain breeze as I heard cows mooing in my front yard. I knew my neighbor's cows take a walk always through the night. I feel blessed to be able to live in this area where life is just like a dream and peace roams around the air.

This ranch life with acres of land had been what I thought to be the comfort and peace my soul so desired, at least as I had thought in those days of my life. Life, however, taught me differently in the years to come. I realized it is not a place, a home, or even the people you surround yourselves with, but destiny that brings peace within one's soul.

As we learn to accept destiny and know we are not destined to our destiny, but we create our own, just be happy that we have tried and the rest is up to The Lord, The Creator. Do not ever give up on any wishes of life for you eventually decide your destiny as you try and achieve or even fail. We learn from our own footsteps as we look back at the footprints on the sand.

This night, I had a very romantic dream, a dream very private and special to my soul. I did have my reservation about writing anything private, but as I am completely honest about all my dreams, I know I had to write about this one. All my dreams scattered all around my dream diaries lead me to this faith that I must somehow make it to this sacred land.

The night was very cold and I was within the warm hands of a special person close to my soul. I saw I was on my honeymoon in a hotel on the top floor looking down at the bottom floor of the hotel. I was there and standing next to me was my husband. I had no clue what his name was or who he was, but knew he was my soulmate. He was as devout as me and believed in celibacy and restraining from all sins of life. This was very simple for us as our first love we agreed was The Lord. Second love was a sacred union with the blessings from the Heavens above.

I was walking hand in hand with my husband as he said they just finished the remodeling of this hotel. It was a newly remodeled Hilton Hotel in Amsterdam, the Netherlands. The hotel was so beautiful with an atrium looking area where we could see the entire top to bottom of the hotel.

I saw we had bathrobes on and a friend had just come to visit us as he had in his hands a Dunkin' Donuts box. He was excited to be able to buy from Dunkin' Donuts. I was shocked why would someone be so happy buying donuts. He said, "Finally now we have Dunkin' Donuts as they have just opened their store here."

I went on a stroll around the town as I walked past historical buildings, tram, and rail systems that were so nice. We had gone all over the city. We had passed some graveyards and I knew my husband's family members were buried in this country as we had visited them all throughout the day. I felt like it was easy to go from one city to another as it did not take a lot of time traveling. It felt like the country was very commutable within a day.

I loved visiting his father's and brother's grave sites as they were close by and we had spent a lot of time there. I had gone to his grandfather's grave site as it was not in the same area. I don't recall if it was in another city or far away from his father and brother, yet I loved visiting all of his forefathers. I recall his grandfather was buried near a huge tree which his grandfather loves being close to. It was strange how I felt like I had known these men. It was a strange feeling as I not only saw my soulmate, but I also saw his family from the past. I knew my husband loved living there and I loved him for that.

I had a very nice time the entire night. As my sleep broke, I was again alone and I did not feel bad as I knew I always saw the future and had a comfort in my heart that one day, I will visit this amazing city. Until then, I will hold on to this special dream. This morning, as sleep broke, I had four different friends call me and retell their Amsterdam dreams of this night.

They had said all of them had seen we had gone to Amsterdam for my honeymoon. I was not surprised with the interlinking dreams because in my life, I have seen interlinking dreams with my close friends and family members even when we are distanced by time and place.

All different dreams of that night from different members of my family and friends had seen a wedding, the newly remodeled Hilton Hotel, and a newly opened Dunkin' Donuts store.

The facts I have only recently found are as follows. The Hilton Amsterdam Airport Schiphol Hotel had her grand official opening on February 9, 2016, but my dream was from 2012. The brand-new Dunkin' Donuts opened their doors to public in the Netherlands in March of 2017. This was very strange as for this dream, I have four different witnesses as they too had seen this dream in 2012.

I had never been to the Netherlands and had no clue about this country which comes in so many of my dreams. This night, however, I had been to a place which did not exist until years later. I had time traveled through my blessed dream and I have my friends who had traveled with me all in our dreams.

We were all shocked as we never knew or thought about considering the dream details until 2016 as so many more dreams were given to me where I had seen the past lives of people whom have matched historical figures as I now have my own dream of the future where I have been staying in a hotel which would not be there until a few years after my dream.

I had traveled to the Netherlands in September of 2017 as I started to write my dream diaries. I just wanted to see this mysterious land with my own eyes, not to prove anything or anyone, but just for my pure satisfaction. I saw in front of me, stood tall and strong the Hilton and all other proofs from my dreams.

I did not have the heart to stay at this hotel as I have found all the proofs of my dream, but him. I enjoyed my trip and know I have fallen in love with this unknown land and the people of this blessed country.

I keep faith alive with me as I know these dreams are talking to me from a sacred land of eternity, where dreams are given for guidance, sailing throughout the dark ocean, always guiding us onto the right path. I don't know what my future holds for me, but I do know I have complete faith in my Creator guiding me today and all from the past to the unknown future through our blessed dreams. For all of whom have asked about my soulmate, I must say he is there somewhere and just like me, maybe he is being guided by his dreams.

My belief is we shall unite one day. I have complete faith in my Creator. Until we meet, though, I will forever be celibate from all known and unknown sins as long as I have life within my body.

Forever, I know all humans in the past, the present, and the future are being guided by this unknown miracle of the night I call the blessed dream. Remember whenever you feel lost or stranded, alone fighting the waves of time, always for me and for you there she stands guiding one and all for eternity, the Spiritual Lighthouse.

CHAPTER

TWENTY-SIX

Where There Is No Hope, There Is But One

"Every child is a miracle complete. Every life is compared to a day. So, wait for this child's miracle to be completed from sunrise to sunrise."

-Ann Marie Ruby

June 21, 2014

Storms come with or without warnings throughout this world and I wonder how we the humans can do nothing as natural disasters but come our way. With advanced technology and so much warnings, we would think we the humans can handle anything. One huge storm leaves us hopeless and we then turn to God for the answers to why my Lord, why was I hurt? Life is a blessing as the storms come to an end for most of us, but some of us live with the remembrance of the storms of life within the sorrows of life. Life, as she has no time for any one of us, walks past us as we are all left within the pages of history.

This night, I had a very strange dream and I have no clue as to why I saw this dream, but I shall keep her logged within the pages of my diaries. It was daylight and the sun was pouring through the beautiful gardens of a small cute house. I saw there was a swing set, a small child's bike, a basketball hoop, and a small midsize family car parked in the driveway. There was a huge tree at the front of the house. Opposite the house was a small park with a children's play area. I watched two women talking with each other as they were pointing toward a house and talking or I thought gossiping in daylight in front of all ears to hear.

I heard a child cry in fear as he ran home and asked his mother what was wrong with him. The babysitter ran after the child as she broke into tears and tried to explain she tried her best, but could not control the mouths of those women who were so insensitive.

I watched the teenage babysitter who was more concerned and had more sense than the two mothers who had everything in life and had no heart for a family who might not be in their shoes. I cried as I saw tears running from my eyes betraying my emotions again. Strangely, I had no clue as to who these people were and what were they going through.

I saw I was walking within a light glowing from the skies, coming through the clouds, streaming within the doors of this house. I saw the mother of this child was kneeled on her knees in front of a Virgin Mary statue as she poured out her tears. She had no clue what was wrong with her son.

The babysitter left as the parents sat with their son, and that's when I saw the boy was somehow different. He started to cry, shout, and jump up and down as his father held him within his arms trying to calm his son down. They had given him a shot and knew the child will calm down as he falls asleep and for a short period of time, he will be normal. The parents knew their baby boy will rest as he gets the shot. I wondered who would the shot help? The child or the parents, as they don't have to watch their son be in pain.

I saw holding my hands were Angels in white and saw their glowing light shining within the house. I asked them, "What is going on within this house?" The Angels showed me the following.

The woman was pregnant with twin boys. When she was pregnant, something happened and she gave birth to only one son.

The child that was born was holding on to his brother's hand as his brother had passed away before birth, yet his soul held on to his brother and was living with him. The child wanted to be born, wanted to play, and wanted his parents to love him too. The parents did not see him and had never known about him, but the child did. He always spoke to his brother and everyone thought he had an imaginary friend. As time passed by, some thought he had a multiple personality disorder.

I cried for both boys as I saw them both always holding on to each other. Both were scared and were lost as they had no clue why no one could see them both. I asked The Holy Spirit for help. That's when I saw the light of The Holy Spirit appear in front of me and ask me, "Why would you like to help an unknown family?" I replied, "But my Lord, my whole life has been praying for all unknown, unseen people as I have complete faith in my Lord whom I see not, but know is there. I have faith in all humans and know at the end, all Your children will come back home to You. Maybe lost and stranded they are, but within Your light, they will come back home."

I asked for intervention for this family as they have no clue what is going on. This child will live his whole life in hiding. I saw that's when two birds appeared in the hands of The Holy Spirit. As He asked the two birds to be separated, I saw the two boys jumped within the hands of The Holy Spirit and He now had two birds in His hands. He let one bird fly away and he placed one back into the body of the existing child. I saw both boys were crying as I watched

The Angels were playing with the boys. The boys forgot all of the sadness and were busy playing and singing with The Angels.

I asked, "What will happen with the children?" I saw The Angels smile as I knew there was a baby boy who will be born into a loving family home. I knew this child will have a completely normal life with new memories, and new chapters will be created within his life.

I saw the boy had awakened from his sleep, and I saw his mother run into his room cuddling him back to sleep. I saw her tears fall as she prayed for her son. She prayed to The Lord. She knows The Lord had taken one child away at birth from her and she knew it was but the will of God, but if it is possible, she prayed that her living son have a blessed life. I knew her prayer was answered today and I felt so good as I awakened from my sleep.

I know The Lord works miracles each day that we are but not aware of. I believe miracles are but within every corner of our lives. Maybe today, your financial problems will not end, or your job application might not be answered, or any other personal problems you and I might have will or will not be resolved. Even though we do not know or see miracles are happening every single day, I pray for this kind of miracle to happen within all the houses of this Earth every day.

I did a lot of research on these topics and have seen a lot of children are born with different problems each day. I believe we need to pay more attention to the children and ask them about their point of view and not let our opinions take over their thoughts.

Children, at a young age, remember much more and know much more as has been seen through research on rebirth and reincarnation. They remember much more and tend to forget as they grow up and time passes by placing imprints of our thoughts over them.

Maybe with more research, we would one day solve all the childhood diseases and eradicate all of them through the miracles of faith and our dreams guiding us through these subjects. For this family, I had prayed as I had awakened for I believe where there is no hope, there is but one, The Omnipotent.

Today, I would ask all of you turning through the pages of my dream diaries, please say a prayer, your own way within your own words, to The Omnipotent for a total stranger with whom you have no bond, but just a stranger in need of a prayer. May all creation of this universe whom but feel lost, stranded, and lonely, even lost and stranded within a house full of family members, know and believe always there from the unknown waiting for all to call her is faith. For when all but is lost and nothing but is found, faith finds you as from the dark ocean watching over all creation of The One Creator, is forever the Spiritual Lighthouse.

CHAPTER TWENTY-SEVEN

Angels In Disguise

"Amongst the stars up in Heaven, we search for them. Yet, as humans amongst humans, appear Angels in disguise."

-Ann Marie Ruby

September 25, 2017

September in Washington State arrives with fall and all her spectacular color changes. The wind blows the crisp fall air through all homes across her land. I always buy the autumn air freshener to freshen up my home. During this time of the year, I open all my doors and windows to let nature into my house. The air had my yogi mind refreshed and after a long evening of meditation, I finally retired for the night. I had yet another strange knock at my door of dreams this fall night.

I was walking at a very fast pace within a cold, chilly night. I had on a blue shawl and was wearing a long maxi dress. I had sandals on which were old and becoming worn out from my long walks. I knew I must keep walking as something was bothering me and I felt like I had a heavy heart within my chest.

Tears betrayed me yet again as they were falling from my eyes even though I had warned her not to show herself. I knew my tears were freezing in the cold, chilly night as they froze on my cheeks.

I started to walk faster as I saw people were not even paying any heed to me as if I did not even exist. I then saw myself looking up at a mountain and thinking if only I could climb up the mountain, I would be able to meet my Lord. I would then ask why my prayers do not reach my Lord's door.

I knew I must climb the mountain and pray for that was the only way my prayers would be accepted. I knew I had enough time as it only takes about two to three hours to climb the mountain and all the people were doing it as groups of people were going up there to pray.

I thought to myself, I would ask for all my emotional pain to be removed as I know for physical pain, I take a pain killer, but the pain no one can detect or see and I can never share with any one keeps on bothering me. I am an introvert. I talk a lot and smile a lot, but within my soul I keep all my pain and sorrows. I believe there is no reason to share all my pain for it will only cause pain to yet another soul.

There in the dark, I saw a child who was about five or six years old come and stand in front of me. She asked me, "I know you are close to God, so can you help me?" I stopped in my track as this was the first time I stopped within my sacred journey. I knew each minute that passed, I would be delayed and then my prayers would not be heard by God. Yet I had no heart to say no to this child and I held her trembling hands as she was shaking in fear.

My heart sank and just wanted to help her. From my soul, I just wanted to know what was wrong? Why was she crying? I asked her to sit next to me in a small craft store as I bought some cold water for the little child and myself. She was hungry, so I bought some bread and butter for her as well. Money was sparse, so I just bought for her as she looked at me with her beautiful brown eyes and worried why I had bought food only for her.

With her mud covered messy hands, she tore a piece of bread and wanted to share with me. So lovingly, she handed me a piece of her bread. I felt like this was the sweetest bread I had ever tasted for it was handed over to me with so much love. I asked her, "Why are you crying? What would you like me to convey to The Lord for you?"

With her trembling little voice, she said, "God would never enter my house, so I want to ask you for help. I don't want this pain anymore. I don't want this as it hurts and I don't like it."

I asked her, "Why do you think like this? God enters all houses and all you must do is pray. Little children are the blessed prayers of this world. All children are heard by God and The Angels of God intervene."

I walked with her and we spent a lot of time just walking and talking. She had played games in the bazaar as other people let us enjoy rides for free. It was getting late and I knew the mountain shall close soon and I would not be able to climb the mountain if I don't leave now, but I had no heart to say this in front of the child. I thought what was this child going through as she was still a baby.

I wanted to cuddle her, give her a warm bath, and place her in bed. I thought where was her mother or father? Why was she so scared and what message was she trying to convey to The Lord? I said to the little girl, "Maybe we can pray together and The Lord might accept our prayers."

She jumped and sat on her knees and held her tiny hands in salutation as she closed her eyes and started to recite with me, "My Lord, help and guide us, for we are the creation and You are but The

Creator. This tiny voice in front of you on this day needs Your intervention. Intervene my Lord and help Your creation."

After praying for a long time with the little girl, I saw The Holy Spirit standing in front of me. Smiling, The Holy Spirit said, "So, you are climbing the mountain for a prayer today. What is it that you ask for?"

I asked The Holy Spirit, "What is wrong with this child? I know her needs are more than mine as she is just a child looking for help. I feel without Your intervention, this child will get lost and another life will be lost. Somehow, some way, my Lord please help this child."

I then saw in front of me, there was fog and within this fog, I saw this child was being physically molested by her own father. I saw the child's mother had left with another man and the little girl was left alone with a man who had no moral values and was hurting this young child, but no one around her was there for her. I asked The Holy Spirit if she had any family member that could help her, but saw no one would help her.

Tears fell from my eyes as then in another fog, I saw there in front of me were some world leaders and their wives walking and trying to help the children all around this world. I had a good feeling as I saw some of these people were doing it from their hearts and some were doing it for the news media and their own publicity. I again asked The Holy Spirit, "Why are these people not being touched by these young lives?"

The Holy Spirit answered, "But they are and that is how The Angels work. Through these humans, Angels work invisibly. There is one such person who is also trying to help as she is touched by these young hearts." I asked, "Who is she?" Then, I saw in front of me there stood a Miss World winner, Priyanka Chopra, walking in a rural village like setting as she spotted this same young girl who was being abused by her father.

Priyanka stopped and watched this child and without realizing, picked this young child up and told her no more will she be in pain. Priyanka told the little girl that she will have help from this day forward. I saw then The Holy Spirit was smiling at me as I stopped crying.

I told the child she will wake up soon from her sleep and will find an Angel in a human form who shall help her and never again shall she be in pain as The Lord has answered her prayers and is sending a great human with a kind heart to her door.

My dream broke and I cried for a long time as I knew I was thinking only about my pain as I went to sleep, but The Lord wanted me to see this little, brave, young heart and pray for all the children of this world. I knew I had no money or physical ability to help this child, but pray. All throughout this day, I prayed for Priyanka Chopra, all the world leaders, and people who have name and fame.

May they be there for all of the children of this world. I am just a human who has only one tool within my hands and that is my prayers and the door of prayers for all the children of this world.

Like all my dreams, I also had looked up Priyanka Chopra and to my surprise, I found she had devoted a part of her life to the girls of this world. She has devoted a portion of her annual income to help young girls of this world. I don't know how I saw this dream and to find out that this person is helping young children brought back all my faith in this world and all the humans who but do help.

I admire these people who are trying to help and I know God works miracles through these wonderful people. Maybe Priyanka Chopra also saw a dream in which she helped a young child who had no other way out. Today, I forgot all about my pain and just remembered the prayer call from a child whom I have never met.

Tears roll down as I could still feel the little trembling hands shaking in fear as nightfall but approached. Let us in union pray for all children of this world to be safe, to have a good meal, and a safe home where they are not violated, but cuddled and comforted.

I felt a warm comfort knowing within the dark night's ocean, The Lord sends to all of us, The Angels in disguise as they appear in human forms. Maybe they will remember the deed or maybe just like the waves, they will forget all about their deeds, yet let these deeds take place and all of us whom can afford, please help. Please encourage all the world leaders, the famous, and the well-known to help the children of this world.

For all of you whom don't have anyone watching over your pain and sorrows, please know from this dark ocean, watching and guiding all the children of this world always is, the Spiritual Lighthouse.

CHAPTER TWENTY-EIGHT

Mother Earth Is But The Healer

"Sacred spiritual healing is but all found hidden within the sacred chest of Mother Earth."

-Ann Marie Ruby

September 20, 2017

Pouring rain calms my mind, body, and soul. I watch the rain pouring into the Puget Sound, as this is the view from my bedroom window. The ferry boats wait to cross people over to the small islands and the horn blows alerting the last call to all the cars and passengers going onto the ferry boats.

The moon shines into the dark water allowing a beautiful reflection of her across the water. The wind chimed a beautiful tune within the air, as she knew sleepless souls await her musical tune to carry them into the mystical dreamland. I always find peace and serenity within Mother Nature, so I enjoy watching her as I drift off to my dreamland.

This night was so special as I had come home from a blessed, spiritual journey through the Netherlands. All day and night, I walked past the memories of this blessed journey. I had gone to sleep with peace and serenity within my soul as my dream had taken over.

I was standing in the dark with the stars as my only guide. I watched the moon above shine and glorify this Earth with her true beauty. I was crying and tears had rolled down my chest as they fell nonstop. I cried as in the dream, I felt lonely and knew I was like an orphan looking for a motherly affection from someone, or somewhere.

My feet were bare and I felt the Earth touch my skin as the water from the ocean washed my feet. The moon shined as I felt all the raw pain of this Earth flood over my soul. Tears fell to the ground

185

and as they touched the Earth, I started to cry loudly. I wanted to get all the tears out from my system. I cried as I saw there were no humans in sight.

I never thought being alone would make me cry as I love to be alone and meditate, and feel God and the presence of God everywhere. I guess I also like being in unfamiliar crowds where I meet up with all different strangers and feel the presence of my Creator everywhere.

After I wept on for what seemed like eternity, a sweet voice echoed in the air. It felt like from beneath the Earth, yet it felt like from above the sky, and from within the ocean. The voice asked, "Why are you crying?"

I replied, "I am lonely and I feel like an orphan. I have lived a blessed life, always following the peace and serenity, avoiding any kind of sin known to me, yet I still feel there are so many obstacles within life. It is hard and at times I feel like an orphan trying to find my parents or I want to know if there is anyone out there for me."

The voice replied, "But, you know I am always there. I have never left and will always be there. I am in the water. I am in the air. I am in the skies. I am in the light. I am in the Earth. All around you, I am. Never my child, are you alone as you walk above me, upon my chest. Know this, I but am your Mother Earth. I am this Earth and all the mysteries are but hidden within my chest. Within my chest, I, your Mother Earth, have buried all the healing ointment for within me, lie all the secrets of eternity. Within the Cosmo lies the eternal truth of all mysteries, not given to the human mind for it is

186

not within the will of The Creator to reveal this truth for the human minds only have what was given to them by The Creator. The Creator has not only created the humans, The Angels, the animals, the known, and the unknown of this universe, but also all that are above and beyond are but the creation of The One Creator. My child, know the truth. If the human creation is but alive, how is it then the humans think all other creation of The Creator are but not alive? If a human only lives a hundred years, how old do you think I am? Are all humans not born from my chest and buried within my chest? Yes, we are all alive my child. The whole Cosmo is but alive and is watching over all of the creation of The Creator. The truth is I am always here watching over you and never have I left you nor shall I ever leave you."

I asked, "Why do I hurt so much?" The voice said, "For all physical illness, you look no further than this Mother Earth. Within my chest are hidden all the answers to all physical illnesses. Try to go outside and stand upon the Earth bare feet. As you meditate, you shall see the healing powers of the Earth heal you. For all other pain and struggles of life, look no further than the Earth, the Sun, the Moon, the Stars, the Water, the Light, and the Air whom but have all the answers of eternity. With faith, and The Creator's will, all is but found. We are all a single family and when you know of this complete truth, you shall be found by us as we shall be a part of your family too. The miracles of eternity shall be known to you with The Creator's blessings."

I said, "When all is but lost and nothing is but found, there from dust to dust, ashes to ashes, from a clot to human, human to a clot, all is but found for there and then my Lord is but there."

At that time, I repeated this prayer for a while as I heard again, "Life is a miracle waiting to happen each day. Even within the dark, remember the sun comes bursting through the night's sky. All the answers are hidden within this Earth and all is but found for the seeker who but asks, seeks, and knocks."

I recited another prayer as I watched from the skies within the dark night appeared the first glow of light as she converted slowly to full glowing daylight. So beautiful is the creation of our Creator. The sunrise is one of the most beautiful works of art within this great world of ours and is completely free and available to the poor and the rich as The Lord is watching over all within the same embrace of love.

I watched the sun rise and saw from the skies, rain drops fell on me. I watched over the Heavens above and told my Lord, "Oh my Lord, this devotee can take all the pain my Lord but bestows upon me, but not the teardrops of my Lord. I promise, never shall I go against the Commandments of my Lord."

I woke up to see Mother Nature was calming the world as it was raining. I knew the rain always had purified my soul. I knew my Lord wanted me to know even though I feel lonely and at times scared of what life brings upon our plates, I must always have faith even when all is but lost and even when all but is gone, there and then stands in front of us our Lord, The Omnipotent.

I know on this day, there are a lot of people suffering from physical and emotional pain throughout this universe. Remember, all the secrets are but within this Mother Earth. The cure for all things are within her and to find this cure, we must have complete faith within The Omnipotent.

I have decided to walk bare feet outside in my backyard and feel the Earth as I meditated taking in all of nature in her true glory. I know within her is hidden all the secrets to a very sacred life, which I call love, peace, and serenity.

Whenever you feel lost and don't feel like getting up to do anything, remember there is someone out there feeling the same way you feel and shares your pain and sorrows of life. Never are you alone. Just gather enough courage to get up and go stand upon this Mother Earth for like a healer, she heals all of whom but ask, seek, and knock upon her.

In my prayer book, I had written a prayer I call "The Healer" for all of you whom need something special. I have incorporated this prayer here.

THE HEALER[5]

My Lord, The Healer, The Omni,

Heal this Earthly body of Your creation.

This world has given illness and

---

[5] From my previous book of spiritual prayers, *Spiritual Songs: Letters From My Chest*

Bedridden Your devotees.

The soul is as always pure and clean.

The Earthly body cries in pain,

Heart cries for You,

Wants to just be in devotion of You.

Earthly body does not move

For it is in pain my Lord.

Cure Your true devotees

For You are The Ultimate Truth.

May we never leave Your Path

Even if our mind leaves us out of illness.

May our pain and sickness

Be wiped away by Your love.

May our prayers reach Your Door.

Heal us for we cry only to You.

Sickness and in health,

We ask You to never leave us.

Oh my Lord,

I know You are The Only One I cry upon,

For You are The Ultimate Truth,

THE HEALER.

Always have faith within your soul, and always know from within the dark ocean, even when all seem dark and lost, watching over all of eternity is always, the Spiritual Lighthouse.

CHAPTER TWENTY-NINE

Prayers Are But The Saving Grace

"Blessings knock upon our doors as an unexpected guest. Have a warm basket of bread and butter ready for her as she but arrives."

-Ann Marie Ruby

July 17, 2012

Cave Creek, Arizona, I had rented a quiet vacation villa by the Black Mountain in Maricopa County. The area was filled with mountain lions, coyotes, and bob cats. I had to keep my puppy within my sight all the time. From sunset to sunrise, I could hear the animals howling as the sunrise was beautiful, but scary at the same time.

I needed a break from this world and all the obstacles of life as I traveled from Maryland to Florida through Arizona. It was a great adventure with so much uncertainty within my life. I decided to rent a vacation villa and take a break from all that life but brings upon my plate.

I did not realize at the time that you cannot run away from any emotional or physical pain for they come to you even though uninvited they may be. You must walk the path of pain and suffering to relieve the pain, as the first step is accepting the pain, and then for physical pain, take a painkiller. For emotional pain, meditate and awaken spiritually as then your soul will find peace.

I had started to meditate at this stage of my life and finally found peace as with time, I realized peace comes from within the soul and it is not found within a vacation villa, or any resort in the mountains or the beach. After I had prayed, I went to bed and had the following dream.

I must say I was totally lost as to why I had seen such a dream and what I should do or should have done. Some of my dreams come with a message and some come as warnings, yet I was lost as to what I could do to prevent these dreams from becoming a reality. All I could do was pray, and my dream from that night is as follows.

I saw a young man sitting in front of his computer angry and upset. He was planning something, but I could not see what he was doing. I saw there was a man watching him who had the face of a beast, yet he looked like a man apart from his face. I saw this beastly man was laughing and calling this young man "Sleeping Beauty."

I saw this beastly man was doing something with this man's head. It was as if this man had no control over himself. I cried and called upon The Holy Spirit to help and guide. I saw in front of me standing were Archangel Gabriel and Archangel Michael. They told me, "Watch." I asked, "Why is the young man not praying or asking The Lord for guidance?" I knew all the man had to do is have faith and pray to The Lord for guidance.

I knew this young man had so much hatred and remorse for himself as he only cared for himself, his feelings, and his way of life. I thought to myself, please have some care for the people around you and all the strangers. I knew people were mean to him and somehow called him a loser.

I wondered why do people bully others and have a direct hand in creating a beast? I thought about the strangers who should stop bullying and give him a helping hand for with a lost soul, we the humans lose a lot more.

I heard the beastly face threaten humans saying he will use this man as he has now given his soul to the beast. I knew something bad was going to happen. What should I do? I asked The Archangels for guidance and I saw there was a prayer written on the paper that I picked up and started to recite.

I had awakened from my sleep and shared the dream with a few of my friends who were vacationing with me. The villa had three bedrooms, one in the roof top area with an open balcony and mountain views. I had stayed in that room alone as my friends had shared the other two bedrooms downstairs.

All my friends had awakened very early as one of my friends was crying for she too had seen a scary dream of the beast and a young man. We had gone out and tried to forget all about the dream. Within just a couple of days, however, as we had turned on the TV, our dream was replaying on the screen. The Aurora shooting incident was on TV and as we watched this tragedy take place, we all froze as if the dream was still alive and walking in front of us.

I saw the shooting had happened in Aurora and a young man who was a loner had done this incident. I cried as to what could I have done to prevent this incident? How could I have stopped this from happening? I had seen the beast call the young man, "Sleeping Beauty," but I did not realize Aurora was her real name until my friends told me after this incident.

We all had prayed and hoped maybe if humans could have faith back within their souls, we would grow stronger together and the beast would be weaker. I knew I could do nothing, but pray. So, I wrote down the prayer I had received within my dream.

194

PROTECTION OF OUR LORD THE OMNIPOTENT, THE ALPHA AND THE OMEGA[6]

My Lord The Omnipresence,

Protect us from all the evil

Within, around, above, and beyond us.

My Lord The Omnipresence,

Keep us safe from all the deadly diseases

And famine that is destined to come.

My Lord The Omnipresence,

Protect us from

All the natural and unnatural disasters

That are but approaching us.

My Lord The Omnipresence,

Keep us within Your hands

As the foreseen calamities

Are but to come upon us.

My Lord The Omnipresence,

When the World but ends,

May we, Your true believers, be upon

---

[6] From my previous book of spiritual prayers, *Spiritual Songs: Letters From My Chest*

The Merciful Ark of our Creator The Omnipotent.

My Lord The Omnipresence, we know

We are but safe within the

PROTECTION OF

OUR LORD

THE OMNIPOTENT,

THE ALPHA AND

THE OMEGA.

I want all the evil of this world that reside within us the humans to be eradicated like we have dealt with diseases that were once thought to be untreatable. Faith within good against all evil will help us overcome these tragedies.

For us whom but foresee the future, we can only hope someday we can all be of help without seeking any attention or being criticized for being wrong or right. I believe I saw this dream as a vision of hope for all creation. I know my Creator wants me to always have faith even through the dark nights as within all of us humans, there is good and maybe we can bottle up this good and spread this all over the world.

I always stand near the riverbanks as I pray for all humans and I know from within the oceans, always guiding all of us is the unknown, unseen miracle of life, I but call the Spiritual Lighthouse.

CHAPTER THIRTY

Web Of The Dragon

"Sweet sin of the deceiver but tastes Heavenly except she is but forbidden. Don't fall prey to this unknown, unseen, mystical sin."

-Ann Marie Ruby

October 21, 2017

I love living in Seattle, yet I miss the Netherlands more than I could have ever imagined. I had a very sacred journey through the Netherlands and as I returned home, I knew life goes on even after a vacation. I needed a break from my vacation through a faraway land who pulls me to her, even within my dreamland.

This night, I had a strange dream where mythology, Abrahamic religions, any religion, or no religion had no difference. The whole world fights over who is right or which group of people will enter Heaven and who will go to Hell. I have my personal feelings as I keep voicing all race, color, and religion, why do we the judged become The Judge? My love for all humans will stay forever even though different race, color, and religion all are humans and the creation of The One Creator.

As sleep had taken over, I traveled to an unknown world where I had no clue why and how I was there. I saw I was walking with The Archangels of Heaven by an ocean. I have been blessed to see them as I know I asked Archangel Michael, "What is happening? Why am I walking by the ocean?" He told me, "Watch."

I saw there in the ocean, there was a huge snake or a dragon of some kind. He was trying to hide in the water as I could see how all would think he was just a huge stone or rock beneath the ocean. He was so big that I saw he was curled up in a half circle shape and his tail had gone all over the Earth under the waters in a circle. I heard The Angels say he was the first to come onto Earth to hunt down all the creation as he had promised to devour all the children of this Earth.

I saw he had a huge tongue which was poisonous and he uses his tail and tongue to catch his prey and poison them one at a time. I watched he was hiding on Earth under the water in a rock like formation. I asked The Holy Angels how to defeat him for how is he all over this Earth? They told me, "He was the first to be upon this Earth and his goal was to poison all humans against each other to only lose to him by becoming evil like him."

I saw The Angels had shown me the only way to stop him is by catching his tongue and his tail at the same time. His head was under somewhere in one country and his tail was in another continent which I don't recall. He hunts through his tongue and tail. I knew this dream had more meaning than I had known and I know the future shall show me the answers. Within my dream, though, I kept thinking the biggest sin is committed through the tongue, but I guess through the tail also. We must control the tongue and the tail to control the sin. Personally, I have seen how words, critically said, are more common than the simple term of appreciation.

My dream had changed and I saw another dream this night. I was sitting in an airport and knew my flight was soon as I was busy on my phone trying to catch up with all my missed messages and notifications on Facebook, Twitter, Instagram, and yes, my emails too. I then saw Archangel Michael was standing there and was showing me a young man standing in front of me who had a dragon snake in a circle on his face. It started from his eyes and went all the way around his nose and face. I was scared this young man would lose all his humanity to this dragon snake as the snake was growing. I started to pray and saw the young man was praying as he saw me praying. Then, I saw the snake jumped off him and was curled up in a circle like a dead worm.

I saw The Angels had smiled and I knew it mattered not what book you follow or what religion you belong to, The Omnipotent protects all as we call upon the same Creator, yet different lips utter different names. I knew evil tried to take over this young man, but his strong faith had him win as he threw the worm off with a knock.

In reality, it is simple as we teach the children never to fall prey for evil and always say no to wrong. I know even we the adults have the same will power and we must know wrong from right. All we need is faith and believe in the power of good.

I woke up with complete faith in humanity and knew if we can love each other selflessly, we could defeat all evil and all of humanity should be completely okay. I searched the internet for any proof of a dragon snake and found out from the early mythologies through the Abrahamic religions, all have talked about the dragon and the snake like animal who hunted for humans from beginning to end. I had described the dragon snake that was in a half circle to my friends and to my surprise, they said in early mythology, the snake was drawn like a dragon in a half circle.

Whatever faith you may believe in, there is only one faith within my book, which is the good, for all evil belong to the bad group. I believe in one religion which I call basic moral values. If you carry them within the basket of your life, you can never go wrong.

Always remember, if you do get lost within the journey of life, take a break and hold on to your basic moral values. You shall find within the unknown ocean, there is the glittering hope glowing and always guiding all toward the right direction, the Spiritual Lighthouse.

CHAPTER THIRTY-ONE

Sin But Spreads Through Generations

"Family tree but carries the traits throughout generations. It is the wise who say always take care and remember to cut off any fungus or it shall but spread throughout all of the branches."

-Ann Marie Ruby

January 26, 2012

Disney World, Orlando, Florida, I had a small vacation home. I wanted to live there forever, but life had other plans for me. Life always amazes me as she gifts me with obstacles and from within the obstacles, I have always found the most amazing rainbows shining through the partly cloudy skies. It was warm and around 60 degrees Fahrenheit this January night. I felt blessed after living on the East Coast all my life, I finally was able to enjoy this warm weather.

I love to watch Mother Nature at night for I feel as though I am her only audience as she displays a different concert each night just for me. I sat and watched this concert of Mother Nature for a long time as finally I had gone to bed. I would love to sit and just watch this beautiful concert as my soul loves Mother Nature and her different colors. After my concert with Mother Nature, this physical body, however had fallen asleep as I had a very strange awakening dream this night.

I was walking through a field and I saw a lot of pine trees and green lawn in front of me. I kept walking as I knew I should have been somewhere and I had to rush. After a long walk, I saw a crowd of people in front of me. I saw there were men and women all shouting at each other. I saw a familiar face as I knew Archangel Gabriel was standing and watching the crowd from a distance. Next to him, I saw Archangel Michael standing and they had more Angels standing with them as they were all watching the crowd.

I saw within the crowd another familiar face and knew in front of me was standing Jesus Christ as he smiled and asked me to join him. He kissed my head and gave me a big hug. I asked him, "What is going on? Why are people shouting at each other?"

He told me to watch as he only gestured toward the crowd. I saw within the crowd, there was a woman who had a child on her lap. She protected her son and told all the people to leave her child alone. The child was scared and was curled up in his mother's arms.

The child was about two to three years of age and I had no idea why people were shouting at this boy. I wondered if we were in a third world country or had we time traveled to the past? I saw Christ had a calm face and such an amazing smile on his face. I was so amazed at the sight of Jesus Christ that I forgot to watch the crowd.

Christ kissed my head and told me, "Look how people treat others if they can only find a negative characteristic." I wondered what was happening and saw now the people were accusing the woman of being an evil, characterless person who had an affair. So, the child was possessed by evil. The child jumped up and down and had tried to kill people even at this young age.

He would run after people with a knife or push them off of a balcony and somehow had done evil to all the people around him. The child's father was standing in the crowd as well and said nothing as the crowd had placed all the blame on the mother. She stood up and said, "In the name of The Father, I promise I was a virgin before marriage and have not knowingly sinned in my life. I don't know

204

why you all are having these weird talks, but my son is fine and these are false accusations."

The mother tried to hide her son's evil doings by pretending they never happened. I saw The Archangels were all watching and did not say anything. I felt so bad and asked for a miracle to take place. I prayed to The Lord, may the innocent be protected and may there be justice. I saw then Archangel Gabriel appeared in the form of a human and said to all, "So you have all decided there was an act of evil done when the child was conceived and that must have been performed by the mother as she carries the child?"

All answered, "Yes." He then repeated, "But, what is your proof and why not the father?" The crowd laughed and replied, "Then the child would be born within another woman's womb."

Archangel Gabriel laughed and said, "So what if I say this child is different? When he was being conceived, his father was having an affair with the nanny who was a whore and had multiple affairs with multiple men. The sin passes on to the woman carrying the child and even though she had no direct connection with the other woman, through the father, she has gotten contaminated. It is said in all the books given to man, do not even think of another person as two become one for from these two, a child is being created. Therefore, there should be no sins involved say the sin is mental, physical, or in any form whatsoever. All children are gifts of The Creator. Do not take this action upon your hands with sin. Go and check with your worldly doctors and they too will share the medical aspects of indirect, physical relationships."

I watched the father look down in shame as he had let all assume his wife had sinned even when he was the only one who could have saved her honor. I cried as I prayed for this mother and her son to be spared from this sin and sinners' touch. I watched the mother had frozen in fear of what would happen to her son and not once did she think of her reputation or what the world would call her.

I saw then a light appeared as I was crying for this family and prayed for the strangers with whom I had no connection. I knew these sins would pass on through generations, as through the blood, people spread viruses and diseases on to innocent souls. I watched Jesus Christ walk over to the child and kiss him on the head. As Christ held the boy, the boy seemed to be healed.

I was watching a miracle take place in front of me. I knew this child and so many others will be healed through prayers. But, I wondered about those children who have no chance as their parents either commit a physical or spiritual sin, and don't even let an unborn child have a chance in life because of their weakness toward sin. I had awakened from my sleep as I cried for all the children of this world who would be suffering because sins spread through generations like a virus.

I did research on this dream and found out medically, it is true. The father having an affair with others during the time of conception or during a pregnancy could infect the unborn child and all the future generations to come. I pray may we the repented, the redeemed, and the awakened not drown in the ocean of sin and sinners, but be saved through the grace of our prayers, by the grace of God, and humans with basic moral values.

May the ocean that surrounds us not be an ocean of sin, but may we be the saving ark, floating to save all of whom ask, seek, and knock for the saving grace. May all pure and clean souls watching out for a miracle find the miracle shining from the ocean onto the lands as the unknown, unseen light glows from the Spiritual Lighthouse.

CHAPTER THIRTY-TWO

The Blessed Power Of Prayers

"Candles burn throughout the dark night's sky for even Heaven above prays as she knows with the power of prayers, dawn but breaks open."

-Ann Marie Ruby

Life is a miracle for we have this day as a gift. "Dawn breaks open through the night's sky," is a phrase from one of my prayers. I always remind myself every day that dawn comes to us as a gift. We must give her back our gift of welcoming her with a prayer, a word of kind notes, or just being there for her and learning the lessons she leaves for us each day. When darkness engulfs all around us and we are left in the dark with no hope, I again recite one of my prayers to become the "candles of hope" for all whom are but left out in the dark.

On this night, as I had gone to bed, I was left with a very strange dream which made my faith in prayers and the miracles of a prayer deepen even more. I always had faith in the powers of a prayer but on this night, I realized these prayers are words from a pure soul to his or her Creator, in any language, form, or way for we are all but the creation of The One Creator.

Sleep had finally taken over my tired soul as these days I had faced a lot of personal struggles and knew I will survive. Tears were my best friends during this period of my life. I never thought this night's dream of complete strangers would make me cry for totally unknown people from across the globe and remind myself people are suffering across the globe and we must all combine our prayers for all.

I walked into an apartment of what looked like a warm Asian country, where all the windows and doors were left ajar. Wind was blowing through the windows as white curtains were swinging in the air. I saw on the balcony, there were flowers of all different kinds blooming fresh sweet scents of jasmine and gardenia into the house. I smelled Indian food and naan bread in the air.

I watched two small children were playing in the living room where they were talking amongst themselves. The girl was about five years old and the boy was about eight years old. The girl was chubby and very jolly. She was laughing and playing while the boy kept sitting down. He was very skinny, tired, and looked somewhat pale in color.

The girl called upon her brother and asked why he got tired. He replied he had no clue. He said, "Not fair. I get so tired and I feel so bad every day. I don't feel like eating and I don't feel good."

His sister hugged him and said, "Let's go pray!" She took her brother to a small enclave where they had Hindu idols. Both children sat and started to pray in their sweet voice as I stood watching them with so much love. I had no clue as to why I was admiring the children. I saw with me standing again was Archangel Gabriel as he was watching them with joy.

I saw the boy had fainted and the mother had rushed him to the emergency room. I watched the little girl kept on praying in the emergency room as the doctor had asked to talk with the mother in a separate room. I watched the doctor being so rude with the mother and had asked her so many questions. He asked, "Did you have any relationship with other men? Have you been with anyone else other than your husband? Do you inject drugs?"

210

The doctor went on and on with his questions. She stopped him and she said, "I was a virgin until marriage. Why is this even relevant to my son's treatment?" The doctor said, "Your husband is one of my regular patients, so I have all the information about him and all the blood tests from him. I need all the information about the mother to treat the child for he is in an advanced stage. How was this not noticed at birth?"

The mother started to cry and asked, "What are you talking about? Why are you talking in riddles? Why can't you just say it?" The doctor then said, "I want to talk to both parents at the same time." The mother told him, "Then, you must wait as even I do not get to see my husband as he is always busy with his work."

The doctor said, "Your husband had come regularly to get his physical and I know he was fine, but I am worried about your health." The woman asked, "What are you talking about? When I had married my husband, my daughter was a few months old and my son was a toddler."

The doctor then asked, "Oh so they are your biological children from your past marriage?" She said, "No, they are my children, but my husband's biological children from his past marriage. His wife was not a good person as they had divorced and she never wanted the children. He had full custody and I had adopted and have raised the children as my own. We have never shared this secret with the children as they were too young and I do not care about biological anything for they are my own as God is my witness."

The doctor then showed the boy's reports as he had HIV/AIDS. They talked for a while as they found out about the biological mother who had passed way from the disease.

The children had gone home with their mother as she had stayed strong. She broke down in front of her husband as he had apologized for his absence. He had only thought about money and work. They talked with the doctors and no one knows how the father or the daughter who was born later never contracted the virus. The children walked to their prayer enclave in their house which they had dedicated for prayers and started to pray.

I watched as the children had seen me and asked, "Are you a Christian or Hindu?" I answered, "I believe in all religions. I also believe in all humans and the blessed power of prayers." I saw the children were watching Archangel Gabriel. The girl asked him, "What is wrong with my brother? Is he dying?"

Archangel Gabriel answered, "What is death? There is nothing such as death. You either be with us like Angels or on Earth with your parents. Either way, it's life, boring and fun at the same time." The children were happy talking with him as I saw then the light of The Holy Spirit appear and asked the boy to lie down.

I saw The Holy Spirit's hands appear as what looked like ice as He touched the boy from head to toe. Then, the hands disappeared and reappeared again, but now they were in the form of what appeared to be a fire, touching the boy the same way. This happened quite a few times. I heard myself praying with all The Angels as we kept on reciting, "In the name of The Lord, The Omnipotent, be healed."

I watched the boy stand up as the hands had left. The children only saw Archangel Gabriel and I who were still standing there. I told the boy, "Ask your mother to take you to the hospital now. You must have fluids in your body as you will have a fever, but you will be completely cured. Always remember the blessed power of prayers is never unheard by The Lord."

The children went to the hospital where the doctor told the parents, "A miracle has taken place! Now the boy has no symptom of anything!" I knew the father thought the doctors had made a mistake.

I saw the children went back home where the mother prayed with her two children in the enclave. She had touched her womb and she knew she was having her third child.

I watched the love of a mother from a faraway land and as I had awakened, I cried and I knew if the doctors would all just be the healers and let their pure hands of healing take over, then this world would have only healers, not doctors of greed, but healers of peace.

I had no clue as to what I saw within the treatment. I had researched and found out nowadays, freezing and heating techniques under medical supervision are being used to reduce fat. Always please remember, my dreams are just that, dreams given from The Omnipotent.

The Lord has given the healers of this world called doctors to heal us, so for any kind of treatment, always be under the blessed supervision of a doctor. Even when you are being guided by your dreams, do share with your medical supervisor for all information as doctors are here to help through the blessed guidance of The Omnipotent.

I tried to do research and have found out medical science is advanced in curing all diseases, but some diseases which we do not have a cure for are only in the hands of The Healer, The Omnipotent.

For all of you thinking about this unknown family, know The Lord watches over all families. Within the eyes of The Lord, a family is made from a bond of pure love. A husband and wife have the purest bond of love uniting them for eternity, and so do a child and his or her parents. No blood can be thicker than love, the pure bond of eternal love.

For all watching out for the purest love and all the miracles of life, always have faith in the words of a prayer. Never feel lost for even when all is but lost, nothing is lost for we are always within the embrace of our Creator, The Omnipotent.

For all of you whom have no faith in The Lord, the miracles, or in any religion, do have faith in yourself for The Lord, The Creator always has faith in us, the lost or the found. It is we who are lost for we are the ones who don't ask, seek, or knock. The Lord is always watching over us from the unknown, unseen place. Even though we see not, The Lord but sees all.

For all of you whom are lost and stranded looking for shore, always know from the unknown, unseen ocean, watching out over all of us and guiding us throughout eternity is the Spiritual Lighthouse.

CHAPTER THIRTY-THREE

Natural, Unnatural Calamities But Awaken

"Throughout the storms of life, hold on to the anchors of faith as you burn candles throughout the dark nights."

-Ann Marie Ruby

August 4, 2013

Long summer nights, the smell of sweet flowers blooming with colors have a natural concert of her own. I sat outside as I watched the beautiful blue skies with a reflection of the sun setting and placing a streak of colors across the world. I love watching the sunset and the sunrise over the vast skies. Any day, I would give up tickets to a worldly concert, be it the amazing or famous artist for whom people line up to see these days. I would give up all of this just to watch my Lord's concert of the sunset and sunrise. Also, amongst my favorite is the moon setting over an ocean. The moon sets at different times, but it always amazes me to watch how in the dark we are left after this miracle.

After my free concert, I turned in for an early night as the following dream had taken over my mind, body, and soul. I believe in the miracles of my Lord in all aspects of life as guidance from the Heavens above.

I saw I was watching the Earth from the skies and somehow, I was watching a country near the Indian Ocean. I knew the country seemed like a square, but was not a square. The country was being shown to me in the shape of a square. Maybe she was mainly square, but had triangles or other shapes which had completed her, but I only saw a part of the country.

I saw I was in the company of The Holy Spirit who asked me to watch. As The Holy Spirit pointed to a spot, I saw the land seemed to be cut in half. It was as if the Earth had broken in half at

217

that spot. I knew it was not visibly possible to see, but also knew scientists have been monitoring all of this from years ago.

We went to another spot where I saw the Earth seemed to have cracked in different places. Again, I knew scientists have known about this and they have been quiet about this for years. We then traveled to another place where I saw the Earth had heated up more than it should be and again the scientists were aware of this. As my dream progressed, The Holy Spirit showed me the sun has been heating up more than normal and no one is talking about it. I saw the sun has been causing a lot more damage than anyone wants to admit in public.

I saw fire all over the Earth, natural, and unnatural fire burning, but no one could control them. I saw tornados, floods, earthquakes, and volcanos erupting all over the Earth. I heard the voices of Abraham, Moses, and Christ warning all humans during their time periods to be aware about this day that shall approach. I saw scientists were worried as they knew something more was happening than anyone wanted to admit.

I saw the Earth was cracking. The crack has happened somewhere, but scientists are not saying this. I saw the Earth spinning. The forces that hold the Earth up were weak. Scientists can see it from space. They are not talking about it. They are thinking the sun has come so close, it is heating up the Earth too fast. They know something is happening. Earthquakes are happening because the magnets are separating.

There are tsunamis and flooding because the magnets are cracking. Natural disasters are happening and scientists know the world won't last. Some are saying one hundred years, and some are saying forty years. Scientists want to say, but the government is not allowing. I knew all knew something was wrong, but it was not in my time. Why should I panic for all knew these were predictions from times ago by all religions, the mythological and Abrahamic, and even science now admits something is happening, but what should we do in a situation we have no control over?

We could prolong things from not happening by being environmentally friendly, but these things were beyond human control or mind. I heard The Angels say, "Where there is no hope, there is but one. Where there is no way, there is but one, for You are The Alpha, You are The Omega." I then heard, "Very soon, he will be born."

My dream broke as I did research. The scientific evidence proved my dream to be true. All the things shown to me were happening and science backs up these natural and unnatural calamities. I also researched what the Abrahamic religions and the mythologies have in common within this subject. They too all believe there will be a miracle, the biggest miracle Earth has yet seen and prophesies about this miracle have been within the households of this Earth from beginning of time to the present days we live in. The only difference is, the prophecies have been made within the prediction of Earth, and her natural and unnatural calamities to have been synchronized at the same time.

The Earth and its current stage match the prophesies made from times ago throughout different religious and mythological houses combined. After my dream, I realized now we have science backing up the period as well. I leave you with the following questions. How do different groups of faith, from the Abrahamic religions through the mythologies, have the same prediction of the End of Time, and the Earth being in this current situation? How did people from the past, with no technology, leave behind their predictions of Earth and her current condition? Why has science with all her technology not been able to stop this condition?

Science can talk about facts, what happened, and what is happening with the help from advanced technology. But, the seekers and dreamers can see the future without any technology involved. How is it that seekers and dreamers see the future without any technology, but science needs technology to see even the near future? When science is backing up a theory that had been predicted by seekers, science has lost the race for the seekers had begun way before and predicted before science realized what is happening. This only proves the mightier power of God, The Omnipotent.

I heard the same prayer being recited by The Angels all night even as my dream broke, "Where there is no hope, there is but one. Where there is no way, there is but one, for You are The Alpha, You are The Omega."

My message from this night is never lose hope even when all seem lost and stranded for always there is hope. Remember, we all came from The One Creator. We are all the beloved creation of

220

our Creator. All shall be okay as even when all is lost and nothing is found, we shall be saved and found by our Creator.

Hope is like an ever-glowing candle glowing within the ocean, guiding all throughout eternity. Always carry hope within your basket of bread and water as you journey through life. Remember always from the unknown, unseen ocean, guiding all throughout eternity is the Spiritual Lighthouse.

CHAPTER THIRTY-FOUR

Deadly Viruses Begin Again

"Cure for all eternally is the beginning, for all things that come to an end had begun somewhere."

-Ann Marie Ruby

July 18, 2016

Sunset over the Puget Sound is a blessed view I have until The Lord wills differently. Life is a blessing and every day I can make time, I try to pray at sunset and sunrise. I am not a morning person and every morning, I have a date with my coffee mug, steaming with hot coffee to awaken me up from my night's sleep.

I could go to bed with a cup of brewing hot coffee and still fall asleep. This night, I had no coffee but fresh lemon water, another favorite drink I have as it refreshes my mind, body, and soul. As I sipped on my glass, I fell asleep and the following dream had awakened me.

I was walking in a group where all the people were really concerned about something as everyone was trying to figure out something or find an answer. Someone was saying, the curse had begun from the times of Adam through Abraham. Life expectancy had reduced significantly within this period of time. People used to live a very long life, but the curse had begun during the time of Abraham as the demons carrying the viruses had released the viruses through mosquitoes.

The well of the Mother Goddess known by the name Asherah had been destroyed and her temples were burned down. I heard within the group, someone was saying, "Even if you do not believe, let The Judge be The Judge." I heard the others say, "As humans, Angels, demons, and fallen angels had descended upon the

Earth, the war had broken between good and evil, and mosquitos were being used to spread deadly viruses."

Life expectancy decreased and all the religions, mythological and Abrahamic, searched for immortality. Knowledge was being burned from all different religions rather than being shared. If only they had shared and combined knowledge, then they could have had much more knowledge.

I saw mosquitoes were being used to wipe off a group or more as humans learned demonic behaviors and used this knowledge against each other. I saw research was being done as to why suddenly life expectancy was being cut so short. Scientists could not figure out why now people have gone from living 800 years to around 100 years or even less.

I saw as time went by, scientists were using mosquitoes for experiments. They have unknowingly released deadly viruses and again harmed the human population. I saw scientists have unveiled through research how a deadly virus was given through mosquitos thousands of years ago. I then saw, recently some scientists have done it again. They were trying to find something and curiosity got the better of them again. The curiosity released this demonic virus through mosquitos.

I saw The Angels say, "Zika virus was totally human controlled experiments gone wrong." They compared the brain of a child affected by Zika virus with what is an unaffected normal brain of a child. They asked me, "Do you understand how different they are? That is what happened from the time of Adam to the time of Abraham to now."

The Angels explained in my dream how Abraham talked about this. Abraham said when people will be born with this type of brain. King David and King Solomon also gave a warning about when this will happen. King David and King Solomon warned you will see it will be just like how dinosaurs became extinct.

Animals were affected first from Heaven to Earth. They could talk like humans, but they lost the capacity. They have the brain, but lost the capacity of human knowledge. They had it, but lost it. Just like that, humans will lose it. It is coming in the form of Zika through mosquitos. They will bring human life to extinction.

There are three types that attack the immune system, through brain, through blood, and through the air, water, and land. The scientists have released this hidden virus into the air of one of the countries. I also saw historians were excavating and unknowingly have unleashed what the prophets had stopped. The curse was stopped, but they unleashed it.

I cried to The Angels for help, for someone to help these children, for now they will have a life worse than any life on Earth. In my dream, The Angels said repeatedly, "When you see these things happening, you shall know, the End of Time but is here." I asked, "But how do we cure these children?" They said, "It is all in the same mosquitoes, the virus and the cure."

I had awakened and had cried for the innocent children who have no say in this situation as they are innocent victims of

225

something someone wanted to test out. I had done a lot of research and have come across some weird reports of research gone wrong on mosquitoes that might have caused this virus. I also saw scientists are trying to see if mosquitoes could be the cure for these viruses.

My message for all of you is, let us unite, all the humans, all race, color, and religion. Let us stand up as one family, one kind, the humankind. It is only then we shall all be victorious. I have a favorite quotation of mine that I always repeat, "Let us work for each other, not against each other." United we the humans shall conquer all obstacles of life. Always remember when and where there is no hope, there is but one, The Alpha, The Omega.

For all the lost and stranded souls, from the dark, unknown ocean, guiding forever as she glows within the dark, is the Spiritual Lighthouse.

CHAPTER THIRTY-FIVE

Heaven And Earth Unite Through The Mystical Staircase

"Climb the ladder to success through the sacred knowledge known as wisdom."

-Ann Marie Ruby

November 3, 2012

Arizona desert and heat wave all came to an end as fall approached and winter was around the corner. I left all my windows open as I turned in for the night. The wind blew in a fresh breeze as she refreshed the whole house. The smell of fresh baked bread and pizza still mesmerized the rooms as I walked to my bed. I had guests visiting and I finally had my alone time. I love to read and just pray as I turn in for the day. I always consider the whole day as a blessing and if morning comes upon my door as dawn breaks open, I shall then pray to my Lord for the blessed new day.

I had a few dreams from this night and will only share one as with all other dreams in which my identity is involved, I would always like to keep my identity separate from my dream diaries. I only want the dreams to be of a guide for you throughout your life.

I saw I was married and had just bought a new house. I also knew I had just been to a funeral and an elderly gentleman had passed away. My husband had kissed my head as he had awakened very early. He wanted to finish some work before the day started. As he kissed my head, he asked me to rest. He said he will be back before breakfast as today, he wanted to make fresh breakfast for everyone. He said he would bring fresh coffee to me in bed.

I jumped up as I knew I did not want to miss even a heartbeat of a minute being separated from him for sleep. He kissed me and I knew I would fall asleep in his arms as he held on to me.

I was sleeping again in my dream as I now saw an elderly gentleman walk into my room and ask me to wake up as it is time. I called the gentleman Big Papa. I knew my father had passed away and I had no clue who this person was. He was chubby, very warm, and had a white gown on. He smiled and told me it will all happen now like all race, color, and religion had predicted. I walked with him and saw some of my family members also walked with him. I saw now we had walked for a while and my husband had joined me within this walk as we now walked up to the top of a mountain.

I saw behind me was our new home we had just bought. Some of my family members and friends I knew were also walking with me. We all stopped at an open, grassy area on top of the mountain. I saw I had told my husband about a person passing away.

I had no clue who passed away, but knew somehow, he was in his sixties and his death was predicted by scholars. Even though it was not a front-page news, it was this death that was predicted from times ago linked to a lot of historical predictions. Somehow, this person whose name was so known to all, somehow was not known to anyone and the death went without notice.

I heard Big Papa say, "Come on. We are late. It shall all start now. Just have faith and watch." I knew I was in a few different places at the same time and was very confused. I asked, "Big Papa, I am married and after these years, I finally have found him, my soulmate." Big Papa laughed and showed me the skies above us. I saw in front of me, there was The Holy Spirit with hands up high, doing something. I saw The Holy Archangels of Heaven were all standing next to The Holy Spirit with their huge glow of light spreading from one side of the mountain to the other.

As the skies parted, a staircase appeared in front of us. It was strange as I thought the entire staircase was made from the glow of The Lord. I saw all The Angels descend from the staircase onto Earth and walk and stand with The Holy Spirit. I then saw someone was announcing names as Messengers of God descended onto Earth down the staircase. I knew Jesus Christ was standing within the crowd and he was smiling at all the people as the mountain was filling up with all different race, color, and religion.

I saw all the Abrahamic Messengers stand on The Holy Spirit's left-hand side. Then, I saw on the right-hand side of The Holy Spirit, there was a huge gap. I saw all the Hindu Gods had descended onto that side. I saw Lord Krishna with his flute stand amongst the Hindu Gods.

I was shocked as to what was happening. Why were there all different religious groups coming down to Earth from the Heavens above? I knew the Second Coming of Christ was upon us and all knew this was the End of Time.

I thought so did we the people change all the religions as we divided amongst each other? I wondered to be greater than all, have we the humans committed the grave sin of becoming The Judge? I cried, oh my Lord, how did we do this and how did we condemn each other to Hell only to be greater than the other?

As all stood, God said, "So let it be! The staircase from Heaven is now formed and let now Heaven and Earth be one as now all The Angels shall descend onto Earth."

I thought about what was going on. How could all different faiths be teaching the same message and we the humans have but changed all the messages to suit our own ways and needs? Have we not had the fear of death or did we think we are all immortal and only our ways are but the truth? I wondered who were the sinners that but changed the ways?

I saw all the Abrahamic group and the Hindu group and I saw so many others standing side by side, yet I knew some and did not know of others. I knew one thing all but had in common was their love for The Lord which was so immense. All had their heads bowed down and hands in salutation. They only had one wish and that was to spread the words of The Creator. They did not want to create a rift.

Not a single soul had fought amongst themselves for power or might, but all had in common the love for The Lord. I watched The Angels descend onto Earth as the staircase was completed. I heard so many names, but could not recall as I awoke from my sleep.

I had today broken down into tears as I had no clue about my soulmate from whom I do get visits in so many of my dreams. I have strong faith and know I will meet him one day as The Lord guides us to each other. Until that day, I hold on to my faith, remain faithful as a human, and keep within my soul, the basic moral values.

I had thought by following the paths prescribed to me by my family and friends, I was being saintly. Why should I be amongst the sinners by accepting all others and their ways of life? I cried as I thought of my great country, the United States. We say in union, liberty and justice for all. How do we follow this verse if we criticize all of whom are not following our path?

To remind us of our pledge, we have the great Statue of Liberty standing tall with a lantern in her hands reminding us of equal rights of all. How can the judged be The Judge and become a sinner? I, on this day, had taken an oath to let all race, color, and religion live in peace and harmony. Let the judged not be The Judge, for I must remember all shall be judged. Let me carry within my soul, basic moral values.

I had never been a very religious person, but just followed my heart and carried within me basic moral values. Today, I started to do more research and have concluded all different religions but teach the same message. It is we the humans who change the message at times because of culture and at times because of lifestyle.

Through periodic times, it seems like the messages of the religions were adjusted to accompany our lifestyle. We have taken religion into our lifestyle as we moved forward with our society. Some of us live to please the others while some of us live to only please ourselves. With the force of might, we change the ways to suit our own needs. Never do we give a thought, oh but there is someone watching over us at all times.

I prayed to my Lord, may I not be a sinner and ignore the message of the Heavens above. I ask all to follow your heart and do as she desires, but please remember not to become The Judge. I believe I have not yet met up with Big Papa, until I do though, I will always have a very soft place for a man who had considered this Earthly child a daughter. I loved having his company throughout this very special dream.

I also had done research and found out like Jacob's ladder from Christianity and the Abrahamic religions, other religions also have ladders and stairways representing the connection between Heaven and Earth. I had done more research as I found out Hinduism uses the stairways to the temples and climbing the stairs as a symbol of union between Heaven and Earth.

Hindu devotees go upon a sacred pilgrimage to Mount Kailash. Mount Kailash, a sacred mountain representing The God Shiva and His Consort The Goddess Parvati, is believed to be the stairway that unites Heaven and Earth. All of this represents the symbolism of the union of Earth beneath and the Heavens above.

The ancient Egyptian civilization also had the pyramids again with stairways linking the same theory of the union of the Heavens above and Earth beneath. I also wanted more proof on this topic and knocked upon the doors of science for guidance. I found amongst others, a Dutch doctor by the name of Pim van Lommel who had done extensive research on near death experiences. Without quoting him, I shall say he and others have done extensive research as individuals have come forward and all claim to say the

233

same theory. All have traveled through a tunnel of light which looks like a ladder, a tunnel, or an interconnecting bridge between Earth and the Heavens above.

Why I had seen this dream I have no clue, but I know within my heart, I shall never divide or become the bridge of separation between my Lord's creation. I shall always be the bridge of union. For this reason, I had published my very sacred prayer book for all race, color, and religion.

May my dreams be a guide and a bridge of union amongst all humans for eternity. My family of humans, Angels, animals, and all of whom but need the guidance for anything within your life, all of you whom are but lost and stranded, please know forever we all have amongst us the spiritual guidance. I call this spiritual guidance my Spiritual Lighthouse, always standing tall amongst the dark ocean, always guiding us for eternity. Never shall any creation of The Creator be lost as always know and believe within your heart, always guiding you eternally is and shall always be the Spiritual Lighthouse.

CHAPTER THIRTY-SIX

Judgment Day—The Bull Of Sin

"Difference between an animal and human is basic moral values to differentiate good from evil."

-Ann Marie Ruby

ANN MARIE RUBY

November 27, 2011

November 2011, I had moved from Maryland to Florida. As I drove into Florida, there was a huge rainbow in the skies and there was a sign displayed in the skies about how Christ is back. I loved the sign and I took it as a symbol of Jesus Christ welcoming me to Florida.

I love the weather and my little vacation house I had purchased to retire in. I thought of moving there as I retire, but life had other plans for me. My life had a big change and as I have kept my private life private, I will say this was one of the most difficult periods in my life. Life could change in a blink and as we the humans are so attached to the ways of life, we take all difficulties we are faced with as a stranger with an agony. This difficult period was a fight with my moral values and what should I do? Accept that I should hurt people and say wrong is wrong and just move on? Or give into my weakness and accept the wrong of others and never say anything and live with this within my soul forever?

I had decided to fight as for the first time in my life, I stood up for myself. I think this was the biggest struggle of my life which turned out years later as I would discover as the biggest blessing of my life. I have lived my life sacredly and have followed the basic moral values of the human soul as I had taken the oath of celibacy from all known sins. So, I have even become a vegetarian. I tried my best to not become the cause or reason of pain for anyone.

236

I had always kept my pain to myself and become a candle for all around me. This month was very hard as I had fought within myself and realized I must move on with my life and not fall prey to the whispers of evil around me. I had taken about another seven months to finally stand on my own feet and only walk for the complete truth.

This night, I had sat on the porch of my house as I had cooked a complete vegetarian Thanksgiving meal even on a Sunday after Thanksgiving as my family members had visited throughout the week. I was shocked to see how much one could learn if only one wills. International cuisine now is available at our doorstep and not only do we have the American, European, and Indian food, but a life full of vegetarian options waiting in front of us. I had a wonderful Thanksgiving meal with my close friends and some family members.

After a long time alone on the back porch, I had finally turned into bed. For my companion, I had on this night my tears as she always betrays me in the dark and spills herself out. I saw a blessed dream and knew for the first time in my life even though all around seem dark and lost, always The Lord, The Creator is always watching over us for eternity.

I saw I was sitting in a room and there was a car in front of my house. I thought I had a huge portico in front of my house where a car had come and parked. I saw a few of my friends and family members had shown up in excitement of a competition going on outside of my house. I stood up and saw I had a white cotton dress

237

on with a blue shawl. I was shocked as how all of this seemed normal and I was not even shocked to see this unknown house or the unknown clothing I had on.

I watched a little girl come into my room as she hugged me and I knew she was my daughter, a toddler. She was so happy and excited as she was having an ice cream date with some of our family members. I had no clue who this child was, yet within my dream, I was her mother and she was my baby. I saw she disappeared with a lot of family members for her ice cream date.

In front of me, I saw from the car a few men had walked into the house and told me they want to show me some things. I never asked them who they were or why I just ran with them. I hugged them and knew their names as I called out to them by the names known to me. I saw in front of me, there stood The Holy Archangels of Heaven.

I walked with them to the car and arrived at a huge stone wall. I walked out of the car and as I hugged all The Archangels. I had asked them, "What have I done in my life to get visits from The Holy Archangels?" I saw Jesus Christ flying over in an airplane as he was dropping something to all the people below the hill.

I watched over the wall and saw there was a huge green field and a hill on the field where humans were involved in a competition of some kind. I asked, "Is it sports day and all the people are busy having fun?" I watched over the hill, people were crying and asking for help. I wondered what had happened as on this day, the sports competition seemed like punishment and all the people were trying to just finish the race of some kind.

The Archangels were just watching and I saw the plane Jesus Christ was in was flying low. I asked, "What is he giving them?" I heard The Archangels say, "He is giving them help, a candy wrapped up in Heavenly grace which would help all of whom have it, finish the competition easily and faster."

I saw Jesus Christ and asked for help for an elderly couple. He said he would help them as he blew me a kiss in the air. I then saw the couple pulling or pushing a bull over the hill. The bull was huge and it looked so ugly and big as if it would not move and they were trying to move holding on to the bull. I asked The Archangels, "What was going on? Who was this bull? Why was the couple trying to pull the bull? Could we help somehow?" The Archangels replied, "We will always help those whom seek, ask, and knock."

I then asked, "But what is going on?" They replied, "Judgment Day." I wondered why the bull was the first one being pulled over the hill. I had so many questions, but they asked me if I was looking for someone special. I wondered who was it? I felt like yes, I was looking for someone, but I was confused as to who it was.

I then saw in front of me a man stood and like so many dreams, he had appeared. I knew he was my soulmate and I would find him as he would find me, but one must not sin and fall prey to the wrong things of life, for sometimes the one we are searching for will not arrive until we have removed all the obstacles from our life. I saw him and knew life after life I would be his for I have faith in my Lord, my Creator. I prayed may my sins be forgiven by my Lord, my Creator, and may my repentance and redemption be accepted by The Omnipotent.

I saw I was within the embrace of my faith and honor. As I watched all the people fight, I knew I would never forget the bull and somehow knew this was the devil who but led all humans astray.

I had awakened as dawn had finally reached my door. I woke up early and prayed as I knew everything in life could wait as all in life shall be lost but our good deeds and the holy prayers of the holy mind, body, and soul.

For all of you whom ask what should we do? How does one pray? My answer is simple. From within your mind, body, and soul, you pray. Also avoid what your heart says is wrong. Just by pronouncing one is right, you will not be right, but by what is right is just that, right, and what is wrong is just that, wrong. We prove to no one as no one can see our sins or deeds but The Lord.

I researched about my dream and found out, yes within all major religions, they do believe in the Judgment Day. I also saw within a lot of religions, they have talked about evil and the bull or the snake and dragon with a bull face. Different religions have different thoughts about evil, but all have agreed upon one truth, good has victory over all evil.

I looked up and found that different mythological groups believe the bull represents sin and in some cultures, evil. Let our sins not become like a bull and may we not fall prey into the sinful ocean of sinners. Always know within us, we always have hope as faith teaches us, where there is no hope, there is always one, The Omnipotent.

Always know from within the unknown ocean, guiding all of us for eternity is the Spiritual Lighthouse.

CHAPTER THIRTY-SEVEN

Judgment Day—The Water Jug Of Eternity

"Water, the eternal bliss of life appears to us when we ask, seek, knock, or even at times when we see her not."

-Ann Marie Ruby

August 26, 2013

Lincoln City, Oregon, beautiful beach and my personal RV. It was a great summer vacation. The quiet nights and strangers parked next to my RV became friends on the go. I felt like I was a gypsy. I had seen so many nice, unknown faces vacationing from around the whole world, including a very kind British couple, a Middle Eastern family, a family from Mexico, and families from all over the United States.

I found out humanity was still intact within the human soul. People were frightened by strangers, yet became so friendly as soon as time had allowed them to remove the veil of fear. I walked under the stars and had my feet become friends with the clear sands. Life had left upon my plate a lot of struggles and hardships. When approached by complete strangers, I could talk about my life freely and had no reservations.

I had told all strangers, I have left my house in Arizona locked up and now was on a journey across the United States trying to figure out the purpose of my life. I told them all about my family, my friends, and never did I feel like I must not talk and hide within myself. I knew it meant I was comfortable amongst total strangers or not comfortable within my own crowd. I realized I needed to find my own comfort and be myself. I realized also it was easier to talk with strangers you know you would never meet up with again. I love nature and the beach as they kept my soul within peace and serenity. I realized houses, money, or clothing can't buy peace, but only peace finds itself within your soul as you allow her to awaken within your mind, body, and soul.

The journey was hard, yet I knew I had a purpose for the journey and my purpose of life is to find peace within the mind, body, and soul. I had moved to Seattle eventually from Oregon and my life had changed for the better as Seattle in her own way had awakened me completely. Oregon, on the other hand, had mesmerized me with her gift of nature, rain, and the sounds of pouring rain and hard wind blowing over my RV. I learned to have faith and just live in peace within the sands of Lincoln City, Oregon.

Sleep overtook my mind, body, and soul as I was transported to a totally different place I could not even dream about, yet I was walking within this place amongst so many different people.

I saw The Holy Archangels walking with me and realized I knew so many of the people within this crowd. I don't recall if I really knew them, but within my dream I knew them very well.

I saw The Holy Archangels had very elegant cloaks on and I was mesmerized by their appearances. I saw within this crowd, walked a beggar who had a torn cloak on and was bare feet. He had blisters all over his hands and feet. I ran toward him as I had a jug within my hands and asked him if I could wash his feet with cold water and if he would like to take a drink of cold water from my jug.

He smiled at me and said, "Yes, I would love to." As he had taken the water, I realized in front of me was The Holy Spirit. I held on to His hands as He kissed my hand. I asked Him why was He dressed like this and how can I help Him. I told Him, "My Lord, I can take all the pain of this world and all that this world can give me, but not the pain or teardrops of my Lord."

He smiled and told me to walk with this jug and see even if my close friends or family members know me or recognize me. For on this day, The Lord walks like this and wants to know if the people but know or even recognize their Creator or is it that they see what they want to see.

I was dressed up like him in a beggar's clothing and walked with The Holy Spirit all night asking people if they would like to take a cold drink of water. The heat above the sky was now boiling hot and the grounds were all dry. There was no water in sight and no one had any drink. I asked my Lord what was happening. He smiled and told me, "Today is Judgment Day for all the people who are but left out. Let us see even in this stage, will they recognize The Lord or just ignore The Lord as a poor beggar?"

We walked for a long time as I saw people had bumped into me and all wanted to avoid the poor beggars as they were scared or frightened or even worried if we had any diseases or something. We told them we are clean and safe people, just poor, but we have water for anyone who wants to drink.

I had the jug with me all night and no one had wanted a drink from me. I was shocked as to why were people not seeing The Lord walks amongst all. Don't judge, but remember you are but the judged. I walked and saw some people had stopped over to talk and one had asked me what it was I was eating and how did I, a beggar, end up with a table, chair, and a bowl full of grapes. I told them I had no clue, but maybe you want to talk to my friend. All the time, they would look at us and walk away. One woman had taken one grape from us and walked past us as she refused to have the cold drink from us.

I asked, "My Lord, what is in this water we carry and everyone refuses?" The Holy Spirit replied, "All the answers of life. Eternity, immortality, forgiveness, and the Door to Heaven are within this cold drink." He showed me all the people were walking with a piece of paper they must get signed and sealed. They were all seeking The Lord and want The Lord to sign their paper. The only problem with this is they must have a drink from The Lord first and then all their papers shall be signed and sealed for they have found their Lord.

I cried as I thought why had I been able to come and accompany my Lord and no one else had stopped or even looked back. The Holy Spirit answered, "Times have changed and people are walking away from The Lord and The Lord's path. They search for The Lord, yet when they see The Lord walking amongst them, they totally ignore." I cried and spoke to The Holy Spirit, "May times pass by me and all this world change, but may my love for you never cease and may this day never come when I don't recognize you."

I cried for all the people and for The Lord as I know The Lord walks amongst all, but the humans don't wait or take time to give grace to The Lord and all The Lord's creation.

I watched The Lord and all The Holy Angels walk all night trying to help all of whom but knock, seek, and ask. My dream broke as I had cried and thought about what had just happened. I have had a blessed dream, yet I was so worried for all the creation of The Creator. People judge on Earth, but would they judge even on the Judgment Day? I cried for a while and I repeatedly recited a prayer I had written.

TEARDROPS OF MY LORD[7]

The sky is clouded with dark clouds,
Raindrops pouring all over the lands.
My Lord, why are You crying?
I pour my teardrops for You, my Lord,
Longing to do the right by You, my Lord.
I want to follow The Path of Your Footsteps.
I wish to show all Your creation
The Door to Your Home.
Even if my walk on Your Path
Seems never ending,
May my tired soul never get off This Road.
My love for You, my Lord, is so strong.

---

[7] From my previous book of spiritual prayers, *Spiritual Songs: Letters From My Chest*

I feel Your Pain for all Your children.

My Lord, I hear You call

All Your children to come Home.

My Lord, You stand at The Door

Waiting for all Your children,

Praying to never let a single soul get off

The Right Path.

I, Your child, keep disappointing You, my Lord.

I, Your child, promise to guide

Your children Home to You,

For I, Your child, can take all the pain

Mother Earth can give me,

But not the

TEARDROPS OF

MY LORD.

I had awakened to a very cloudy sky where all the people were pulling in from different cities and different places. I walked in the rain, on the sand, and saw there was no one on the beach. I knew Lincoln City was also known for gambling which I could never do in my life. This is just a way of life for me and never shall I condemn the ways of other people for all people have their own ways of life.

I knew The Lord is watching over all the creation, and the love for the creation is so much that even on The Judgment Day, The Lord still walks to save even one more soul.

The reason for my dream I have not analyzed. I try not to think about these answers, but I pray for all people to have mercy for one another and may I never be so lost in my own world that I would be lost from even my Creator. May my path always be of peace and harmony.

For all of you thinking what can we do and how could we be closer to our Lord and be a sin-free soul, I ask all of you to find yourself first and then you shall find The Lord. This world has blessings from the Heavens above as Angels roam around in human form and always know around the corner, there just might be an Angel in disguise.

Be kind to all and even if you fear the stranger, please do not be mean or unkind. The complete truth always stands in front of us as we awaken each morning and as we turn in for the day. Always guiding all lost and stranded souls from the faraway ocean is always the Spiritual Lighthouse.

CHAPTER THIRTY-EIGHT

End Of Times, The Dark Ages Again To Come

"The ocean, the land, and the skies are but filling up with sin and sinners. Take a bath within the springs of repentance and become the life saver for all."

-Ann Marie Ruby

July 13, 2013

Butte, Montana, beautiful city and standing tall within this city is the Virgin Mary statue. I was on a cross-country summer vacation with a few friends with our own RV. We had our house on wheels and the best part of this journey was we stopped and did sightseeing as we had desired. We rested for each day at sunset as my only request was not to drive during the night hours.

We had stopped and all of us admired the Virgin Mary statue and the city lights glowing all around her. I was in so much peace this night as I had turned in early. Our RV had sleeping arrangements for eight people and there were five of us. I had my own sleeping quarter with a queen bed and wall to wall glass windows on both sides. As I had turned off all the lights, I could see the entire view from my bed. The skies and the stars were so visible. I had prayed to my Lord and fell asleep even though I wanted to enjoy the view all night long.

My dreams of this night had left me with a shivering, cold feeling as I thought the air conditioning was running on high. I was watching a mountain and I saw a lot of people were gathered all around this mountain. I wanted to get a closer look at what was going on as I saw people running away from the mountain. There were cries and fear rocking the air. I walked closer to the mountain as it was then I saw there on top of the mountain was standing The Holy Archangel Gabriel. I saw Archangel Michael and other Angels were all standing in union.

I heard the voice of Archangel Gabriel sound in fury as he said to all the people below, "This time it shall be greater than Sodom and Gomorrah, for your sins have become greater and now you all change the laws of the land to suit your needs and your sins. I say stand in front of me and justify your wrong, your selfish needs, against the words and the Commandments given to all throughout time. Your will prevails because you all sin and you make it justified because all are being unfair and unjust to your needs. What of the needs of God, and the words of God?"

I heard his voice as he said, "The lands shall be flooded. The Earth shall rip open and you shall face natural and unnatural disasters as punishments. All shall see the wrath of God and you shall realize the punishments given before your times are nothing compared to the punishments yet to come."

I cried from within the crowd and started to pray to my Lord. I placed my hands together and prayed nonstop. I cried and repeated, "But I am still here and I pray each and every day. I avoid sin and I never judge anyone for all shall be judged by their own actions." I cried and asked, "Why should You see the sins and sinners, but not the prayers of a devotee and a repented soul?" I cried, "Does my repentance and redemption not reach Your door?"

I saw in front of me was standing The Holy Spirit and He was smiling as He answered, "Yes all the prayers of a repented, redeemed, and pure soul do reach the Doors of Heaven, yet the predictions of the End of Time have begun as it is now the sinners whom have no fear. They live for this life, only to please themselves, and be accepted not by society, but they change society to be like them, so all their sins are now justified."

I knew there was no reason to fear or cry for the End of Time must be as it had been forecasted by the past to the present, and throughout the future, this stays with us. I cried as I held on to The Holy Spirit and I promised Him, "I shall stay sin-free and I shall see to it that during my time on Earth even if I could, I would have at least one other soul repent, redeem, and awaken sin-free and show even at the End of Time, there are sin-free humans waking up with the sunrise and sunset."

I watched a map and I knew the disasters had started and people were losing their homes and family to floods, earthquakes, hurricanes, and other calamities beyond human control. I saw Angels walking all over Earth and they too were shedding tears as how and why have humans forgotten the Commandments given to all race, color, and religion.

I watched people from the Abrahamic religions trying to hide within their churches, mosques, and synagogues. I watched Hindus repeating Kaliyug as they turned to their temples, a word which means the dark days of immoral value are but here.

I asked The Holy Angels to intervene for us the humans. I prayed nonstop all night within my dream and as I woke up from my sleep, I still saw the vision of The Archangels standing up on top of a mountain and promising this time, it shall be worse than Sodom and Gomorrah.

I did research as I had awakened and found out all different religions have proof of the End of Time being a curse from the Heavens above. I had also looked into science and found out even scientists are baffled as to what is going on with the weather patterns, and all the natural and unnatural calamities that have arrived without any warnings. Even though science has improved so much, we still cannot prevent all of this from happening.

I had written a very special prayer after this night. I prayed nonstop for all the humans, the sinners to repent and the repented to be saved.

FORGIVENESS, REDEMPTION AND AWAKENING[8]

My Lord high up in The Heavens,

Your world has manifested in sins.

All around me,

Your creation has become full of sins.

Thus, dark souls surround me.

I walk amongst the sinners.

The sinners have made me into a sinner.

Forgive me my Lord.

Forgive me my Lord.

---

[8] From my previous book of spiritual prayers, *Spiritual Songs: Letters From My Chest*

Forgive me my Lord.

My Lord, the souls of Your creation

Have become dark.

The rivers and the oceans are filled with sins.

The deep water is drowning me in the river of sins.

My Lord, I have become manifested with sins

For all around me,

There is nothing but waves of sins.

My Lord, with hands held up high,

I ask forgiveness for my sins.

Pull me up from the ocean of sins My Lord.

My Lord, forgive me.

My Lord, forgive me.

My Lord, forgive me.

My Lord, I am drowning in this ocean of sins

And I cannot come out of it for all around me,

Souls have become dark and dingy.

Pull me up for I see the shore.

I feel the mountain breeze.

I smell the spring water from the mountain.

Cleanse me my Lord with the mountain waters.

Pour the raindrops all over me.

Wash away my sins my Lord.

Cleanse me my Lord.

Cleanse me my Lord.

Cleanse me my Lord.

Forgive me my Lord.

Forgive me my Lord.

Forgive me my Lord

For sins have manifested

Into the deep waters of the ocean.

All around me, the waves of sins

Drown me my Lord.

Hold my hands my Lord.

Hold my hands my Lord.

Hold my hands my Lord

And pull me out of this ocean of manifested sins.

I am drowning my Lord.

I am drowning my Lord.

I am drowning my Lord.

I see my Lord upon the ocean

On top of a bed of water.

Sins flow in the water,

But the sins do not see or touch my Lord.

Forgive me my Lord.

Forgive me my Lord.

Forgive me my Lord for my manifested sins.

I will walk for my Lord

Through an ocean of poisonous sins.

The love for my Lord is so great,

No sin can touch me or drown me.

For my Lord, I shall give my life.

For my Lord, I shall give my life.

For my Lord, I shall give my life.

My Lord picks me up

From an ocean of sins.

No sin shall touch me.

No dark, dingy soul shall come near me

For we, the creation, ask and my Lord forgives.

My Lord calls upon all the creation.

It is time we, the creation, ask for

FORGIVENESS, REDEMPTION,

AND AWAKENING.

FORGIVENESS, REDEMPTION,

AND AWAKENING.

FORGIVENESS,

REDEMPTION, AND

AWAKENING.

I know all of us only want what is good for each other. I will always pray for all of us, the divided religious groups to be united within one house, I call the house of the repented and redeemed souls. May all of you whom are still looking for an answer from within your soul find it inside your soul. May the blessed ocean of knowledge give us the lost and stranded, hope toward a blessed future. May we find within this ocean, the guidance as always from the unknown ocean, guiding all lost and stranded souls is forever the Spiritual Lighthouse.

CHAPTER THIRTY-NINE

Eternal River Of Life

"Reincarnation is but the spiritual and physical awakening of the mind, body, and soul, like the river water after her time but converts into the clouds, then rain, and again flows into the river."

-Ann Marie Ruby

February 3, 2013

Route 66, was one of the roads I loved driving on. I lived in Arizona and every day at sunset, I loved to go out for a quiet drive. There was so much history along this route, I felt like I lived within the memory lanes of history. The past, the present, and the future become one through this connecting road. After living on the Eastern Coast of the United States all my life, I loved this new-found land which gave me a home on the range.

Five acres of land with fresh vegetables and cows roaming around like I had deer in my Maryland home. Roosters wake up the neighborhood letting all know dawn has approached. Life I had finally taken with a breath. Do you ever have the feeling we are always holding our breath and just try to go on? I had that feeling exhausting me out. Arizona was a nice break from my marathon of life.

February is a nice refreshing time for me as I look forward to spring and realize the cold winter and all the dark nights are about to end. Nature is my favorite teacher. I feel like I am her favorite student. I had the fire cracking and a fresh pot of lemon ginger tea brewing, as I always drink lemon ginger tea all throughout winter. I had decided to turn in as the following dream had taken over my mind, body, and soul.

The sound of water, the force of the sound was so loud, I felt like I was walking within a river. I opened my eyes and saw there I was knee deep in the river. The water felt so nice, I just wanted to stay within her chest. I felt like I was within the embrace of my mother and the water was a shawl wrapping me up in a warm blanket, as she protected me from all obstacles of life.

My feet were bare and I had a blue shawl and a white dress on. I was shocked as to where was I, and why my clothing felt like from a movie set. I prayed as I held on to all my thoughts. The feeling was mesmerizing and so meditative, I wish I could have bottled up my feelings and given it to all of you. I felt this glow of heat radiate to my body as I finally opened my eyes. I saw there in front of me was a light glowing on me like a miracle.

I heard a voice say, "So you are awake? Are you ready for your next journey?" I answered, "Yes, I am ready and is this my last life? Will I meet him in this life or do I have to wait for another birth?"

I heard the voice say, "Yes." I asked again, "So yes I will meet him or yes I still must wait for him or what?" The voice said, "This is it. So, in this life, you must cross all the obstacles and know, throughout all the pain, it shall finally be. You shall meet your soulmate in this life even though life might test both of you. You shall endure obstacles and the union shall be." I asked, "So is the dragon captured who has been separating soulmates and has created obstacles ever since he has left Heaven? Has the savior been born? Has the savior returned? Or what happens now? Are people still circling the circle of life?" I heard the voice say only that, "All shall be victorious."

I saw I had walked out of the river of life and I knew I had done this repeatedly, but this life would be it. I will find him in this life. Within my dream, I kept hearing about the War in Heaven and how The Archangel Michael has been engaged in a battle with the beast. I knew the beast had run after the children of God and all on Earth must not fall prey to the beast.

I was walking for a long time as I ended up in a mountain spring and had taken a shower. I saw I had fruits and coconut water with me. I knew my journey was going to be very hard, yet I must continue this journey.

I prayed along my journey as I saw others walking as well. I asked the river of life to help me one more time as I shall always awaken for only my Lord and I shall always be truthful and devoted to all the Holy Commandments. I saw the light shining from the Heavens above onto Earth and the water looked blissful. I knew I would be okay and at all crossroads and as obstacles come upon my path, my Lord would always be there. I prayed, "May my Lord's will always prevail."

My dream broke as dawn had approached with the music of roosters singing to let all know it is but dawn. I had awakened and prayed to my Lord for guidance. I had not believed in reincarnation, but I considered this theory. I found out early Judaism and Christianity had reincarnation. Within Hinduism, reincarnation exists and is believed to be a part of their fundamental beliefs.

I had once again searched into science and found out science can no longer reject the aspects of reincarnation as too many proofs have been found within this subject. If a few cases could prove this subject, then science has proved that reincarnation does happen. Stories of people remembering their previous lives and going on a tour to find proof for themselves have resolved many cases as they have also aired on popular news shows on the television.

I believe each mind has its own rights and belief. If only we carry within us the basic moral values, we shall all coexist in harmony within our own faith.

My dream from this night I have no clue, yet I did have a hard life. I still am blessed to have this life for as each day I awaken from sleep, I know I have yet another day. I still search for my soulmate, but I know life is a blessing and I shall always live by the laws and Commandments of my Lord, and I know all shall be well.

I know for me and for you always guiding from far away within the dark ocean is always the Spiritual Lighthouse.

CHAPTER FORTY

Spiritual Lighthouse

"Spiritual souls seeking solace eternally, remember to search within your soul, for within each sacred soul glows eternally the Spiritual Lighthouse."

-Ann Marie Ruby

July 1, 2017

Seattle, Washington, my home. The Puget Sound, the Olympic Mountains are the perfect view all around my house. Rain pouring so ever gently and the wind blowing all the windchimes set the perfect orchestra for the concert taking place outside my windows. Children playing late through the summer nights remind me I was a child once and staying up late was a treat for which I would do any chore. Tonight though, I enjoyed Mother Nature with all her wonders of life.

I love the musical rain as it reminds me of a girl dancing with joy, bare feet, and not worried about all the obstacles of life, but just the love of life. I was that girl, never worried, always carefree, and I never had wanted to think of tomorrow. My favorite line as I was a child was "Tomorrow never comes." Tomorrow had come as it became today and life continues with the joys and sorrows of life.

I have learned to live life as life lets us live her. One thing I have learned though is I can't stay up late anymore and I must turn in bed as sleep comes and takes over my body.

Tonight, I found myself in a glass room with olden layered brick work all around. There was water outside as if this building was floating in the ocean. Everything was dark outside and I saw it was a beautiful clear night. I saw next to me were a few gentlemen who asked how does this feel. I told them this is so amazing, I really don't know where I am, but I never want to leave.

They laughed and hugged me in a group hug. I saw The Holy Archangels of Heaven, The Archangel Gabriel, The Archangel Michael, and more who were standing amongst this group. I felt like I was amongst family. I wondered, where was I? I was standing in a glass room where on the wall, was a screen, and on the screen, was the map of the whole world and beyond. I jumped up and down as I just knew I was in the Spiritual Lighthouse of The Lord. The lighthouse was floating within an ocean and it was moving like a boat. I saw from the sky, a light appeared onto the lighthouse. As the lighthouse started to glow, I saw there were so many boats coming and going from the lighthouse. I knew they were all the boats carrying the dead and living people to be taken to their destination.

I saw little babies being carried by Angels to their destination of birth. I saw people of all ages were being brought back within these boats. I heard people were singing in joy as they were all excited that they have finally reached their destination. I saw The Archangels watching the stars as I asked, "What are you all waiting for?" They replied, "It's almost time for the birth and with this sacred return, all humans are saved."

I watched all the light from Heaven glow through this lighthouse onto Earth through the glass, through the ocean to the other side. I saw this lighthouse was spreading light throughout the dark and throughout the nights.

I had asked, "How long would this lighthouse shine upon all humans?" They answered, "Until the son is born." I had seen The

Angels all singing in joy as all is well for all the humans who but want to be saved shall be saved. The boats kept leaving the lighthouse as they picked up passengers to and from.

I asked, "What of the people who need help in health, wealth, or wisdom, or just need some support from the Heavens above?" They answered, "Always, a boat is ready for intervention." I saw the love of all The Archangels for the humans was so much. They had been just happy to be there and help each and every one of the humans. I compared them to lifeguards.

I asked them, "Would you only save one group of humans and let all others to be extinguished?" They replied, "Not in the Heavens above, as a parent loves all of the children the same. How can they not?" So, I asked them fearfully, "What about different religions?" They answered, "In our eyes, there is wrong and there is right, and in between we have a classroom full of children for the ones who choose to learn, they learn and repent."

I hugged Archangel Gabriel as I started to cry. I asked him, "But how do I help you? How can I be of a help? All of my life, I have prayed to my Lord for help, but on this day, I would like to be of help for my Lord." They asked, "Have you written the songs yet?" I answered, "Yes, I have and I know I have the courage to talk about all of my dreams and may all of whom are seeking any kind of help, find it within these pages."

They told me all we could do as humans is pick up each other when we fall and always know to never judge, for the judged shall not be The Judge.

266

I watched all the stars were blinking in the sky as the lighthouse glowed even brighter as she spread all throughout the Earth her light. I knew all day and night, The Angels were roaming around this Earth to help us the beloved creation of our beloved Lord. I prayed all night for all my Lord's creation. The stranded bird or the stranded human, may all of us find our way back home.

My dream had broken as I knew I must write this book and publish it. I know I must cross this ocean of fear and write my dream diaries. Life is a test for all the humans. I know we are standing on top of an ocean going through a storm. May we hold on to each other and cross this ocean together. Different race, color, and religion we belong to, yet we all belong to the one Creator.

This was a very sacred dream as the feeling within the lighthouse was an amazing feeling I wish I could bottle up for all of whom who but seek this peaceful serene feeling. I have finally found a way to bottle up my love for all of you whom seek this serenity. I give you my Spiritual Lighthouse.

Throughout your life on Earth, never give up on faith, hope, and love. Remember The Creator loves us so much. We are always being guided throughout eternity. For me and I know for all of you, always within the dark ocean, glowing in glory as she lights up, and guides all throughout eternity is the Spiritual Lighthouse.

For all seeking a prayer to recite in union, I give you my "Spiritual Lighthouse."

SPIRITUAL LIGHTHOUSE[9]

My Lord, my Creator,

From the first dust of dawn, through the dark night's end,

Through the ocean full of obstacles,

We journey only for You.

My Lord, my Creator,

The journey of life begins and ends at Your command.

My Lord, my Creator,

All of my Lord's Angels from Heavens above

And Earth beneath hold on to the Ark of my Lord.

The blessed messages of The Creator are but spread

Amongst us the creation throughout eternity,

Only by The Blessed Angels of Heaven.

Oh My Lord, my Creator,

From The Heavens above onto the oceans below,

Guiding throughout eternity,

Throughout all the obstacles,

Throughout all the darkness,

Throughout all the hurdles,

Guiding one and all of Your creation,

Forever and eternally but is,

My Lord, my Creator's

SPIRITUAL LIGHTHOUSE.

---

[9] Exclusively written for *Spiritual Lighthouse: The Dream Diaries of Ann Marie Ruby*

I had this blessed dream as I had decided to write my dream diaries. I have had quite a few dreams of being in a lighthouse with The Holy Spirit and The Holy Archangels of Heaven. I had never realized the significance of a lighthouse and religions until I had these dreams and finally searched my favorite search engine and found out my dreams had much more in depth than I could ever think. I have been blessed as all the names of my books have been given to me within my dreams as was this blessed book.

I have found out through my research the lighthouse had appeared from mythologies to Abrahamic religions as an ancient symbol. It reads as follows in the Bible,

"Ye are the light of the world. A city that is set on an hill cannot be hid. Neither do men light a candle, and put it under a bushel, but on a candlestick; and it giveth light unto all that are in the house. Let your light so shine before men, that they may see your good works, and glorify your Father which is in heaven" (*King James Version*, Matthew 5:14-16).

Blessed be the holy dreams given to us the humans by The Creator of all mankind. We must know at the end, all shall begin again as The Lord shall walk amongst all humans. We the saved, repented, redeemed, and awakened shall be guided back to The Creator as we are guided from, by, and into the Spiritual Lighthouse.

THE FINAL CHAPTER

Dedication

"Sacred dreams of the sacred soul create the destiny and destination of the sacred seeker."

-Ann Marie Ruby

December 10, 2017

Dedication is a very personal aspect within my soul. When you fall in love, you dedicate your complete soul to the other person, to the other soul, who reciprocates the same feeling. Love is a two-way street where there is no give and take, but complete oneness. What happens when there is no other person or the subject in question is but unable to talk, walk, see, or feel? What happens then?

I believe there are in some cases the complete giving of love, like a mother's love where love grows even more just by giving. For me, love is very different as I believe love always is the most sacred prayer of eternity. Love for me is but the first dew of the morning, the first peak of dawn, Mother Earth pouring her heart for her children.

Strangely, I fell in love with an unknown, faraway land. Within my eyes, this is a very sacred land. All throughout the night, she spreads sweet fragrances all over the world, as her beautiful flowers bloom throughout her chest. Flowers sing the songs of union as the charming windmills, standing tall, capture her love and keep this beautiful land in union for eternity.

The windmills whisper stories from the past to the present through the future. Within this picture frame, the faces change throughout time, but The Creator, the artist of this canvas and The Creator's art, this beautiful sacred land, remain the same. I call this land a sacred dreamland where my dreams have taken place throughout time.

The artist of this romantic land of flowers had given me the pleasure to have witnessed this land within my dreams, the reason being known only to the artist, The Creator of all land and all creation. I have dedicated my book to a sacred country who had visited me, an unknown stranger, throughout my dreams. Through these visits, I have adopted myself to this land. I know her like I know how to walk through my house in the dark. I have walked with her throughout time.

I asked myself repeatedly if it is possible for a land, a country, to have a soul. My heart says yes, but I know each one of you have a different answer for this question. I know my dream diaries would not be here if I had not found her or the special visits from her.

For this, I know she is the sole reason for the birth of my dream diaries. I had acquired the courage and wisdom to speak about my dreams and faith within all religions as I had the blessed dreams of a very sacred country. From her history throughout her present times, I have witnessed her stories within my dreams. Never had I laid my feet upon her chest, yet she came to me throughout my dream diaries.

A faraway land, a country not my motherland or my adopted motherland, but I feel her soil touches my soul and I had awakened as if I had taken rebirth. I am a child who loves this land even though she is not related to me in any physical form. I feel as though I could touch her within my soul and when I walk through her history, matching my dreams, I feel blessed as I finally realized you don't have to be related or have a physical bond to love or just be happy for the ones, or in my case a country, a land, a faraway mystical land from within my dreams.

I felt for her like she was my mother. It made no sense, but within my heart, it did. I know why so many poets have written songs and poems comparing the land and the soil they were born from with a mother.

I had dreams where this land stood asking me to visit her as she is where I must be. I stood upon her and the rain washed me as I knew there was magic in the air. I wanted to travel to this land even if I could be there for a day to see her in person before I publish this book.

She is a land where rivers flow throughout her like honey. Cows graze around the green fields as they share with all, their milk, butter, and cheese. Wheat spreads her seeds all around as she fills the air with the aromas of fresh baked bread. The carpet of tulips gathers all the memories of sweet love as the windmills spread their sweet love songs throughout history. This is but all within my dreamland.

You know her by her given name, the Netherlands, or as the locals like to call her by her other name Holland. I have adopted this country like a mother even though she is not my birth mother or adopted motherland, yet within my soul, she is my mother as we share a sacred bond. Forever, I shall remain a well-wisher of this sacred land. With the peak of dawn, I pray for this land and as the sun sets and we are left within the dark, I pray for her to be safe and keep all her children safe within her chest.

I know every time I hear any news about this land, I panic and start praying may she be safe, may her children be safe and be happy. May my prayers reach her door, and may my love keep her safe. All throughout my book, I have talked about my personal dreams and the journey of my life as I have taken you on a journey through my dreams into another parallel world. Within this chapter, however, I have taken my dreams and traveled through this world, this land, and allowed my parallel world to be my guide as I be your guide throughout the Netherlands.

Dreams are given from the Heavens above to Earth beneath for guidance. From the Abrahamic religions to the great mythologies through the scientific research, dreams exist as dreams are the guiding lights of eternity. I compare dreams to the eternal lighthouse of each soul. Throughout this chapter, I walk through a country unknown, unseen, and unheard as she was to this Earthly soul. Wonders of this world are buildings, landmarks, pyramids scattered all around this globe, yet within my soul, wonders or miracles of this eternal life lie within a land, a country where all my dreams had begun.

Walk with me through my dreams as I walk upon this sacred land which came within my dreams. Life is a blessing and only shall the future tell us the reasons for these dreams who have talked to me from the yesteryears to the present times to the years yet to come. May we all be guided as we walk through the journeys of our lives.

May my dreams be like an anchor of faith, belief, and wisdom to all of whom seek, knock, and ask for guidance from our sacred dreams. Take my hands through this last chapter as I walk you through "The Final Chapter."

Before I sent my book out for publication, I decided to visit this country in person as my soul wanted to see this amazing land. I finally had taken a sacred journey through a sacred land where my mystical dreams had taken birth. I felt alive as I took my first step and laid my eyes for the first time upon a mysterious land far away from my home.

In person, I saw so many of my dreams standing in front of me, yet times have changed. The buildings, the bridges, the castles, and the hotels all were standing in front of me. I wonder how am I connected to this land? How is it possible to have this sacred bond with a country I had never stepped upon in this life, or does our soul time travel through dreams yet to places we will visit or is it possible somehow my soul was there? I believe in reincarnation, a touchy subject I never believed in, yet life has taught me differently. I do believe in reincarnation as not only different religions, but science has evidence of this theory to be just not a theory but a reality with which thousands of humans but live.

Was I here during my past lives? Will I be here in the future, and just maybe have a future with her? Maybe my soulmate walks upon these lands and I see through his eyes as I believe in soulmates. Only time will tell, but for now, I am happy I was able to travel to this blessed land.

Weather forecast throughout my trip would be rain showers, cold, wind, and maybe slight breaks in between for the sun to play peek a boo. With complete faith, I had started my journey, and I knew my life always had an obstacle stored for me at every corner which I have taken as the teachers of life. Sacred journey of life is just that, sacred, and within this journey, we have complete faith and hope as our guide. I always carry with me love and tears as I know these two are but each other's consort of life.

SeaTac Airport, greater Seattle, Washington State is where I had boarded on a Delta/KLM direct flight to Schiphol Airport.

Amsterdam, the Netherlands. Nine-hour time difference did not seem bad as I had traveled to places like India which had almost a twelve-hour time difference. I have been a world traveler, so traveling was easy as this was also a direct flight which I enjoyed so much, especially for the cabin crew who had gone out of their way to make sure I had diabetic friendly, vegetarian meals.

I was shocked how they ran after me and had brought packets of diabetic sweetener to take with me for my trip within the Netherlands. The crew member told me he was worried if I would be able to find some diabetic sweetener, so he wanted me to have some in the case of an emergency coffee urge. I guess you now realize, I had coffee non-stop as I love my coffee.

I was in tears at this kind gesture from an unknown person. I will forever remember him within my soul. I had given him an American hug as he laughed and hugged me back. As I was walking out of the airplane into Schiphol Airport, another crew member hugged me and said welcome home. I had chills down my spine as that is what I had seen in so many of my dreams. Some life, sometime, maybe years ago, maybe in another lifetime, only truth knows the truth, but I felt like this land was, is, or may be my home in the future. Time is only a secret and answers are left within her chest.

A country I had never been to, yet she had come within my dreams from the year of 2011 to the year of 2017. The land of my dreams, where for me the miracles have stood in front of me and have spoken through the stories of the past to the present and yes, sometimes I had been given dreams about this country before she herself had seen the wagons of life take the effects of reality. Within these years, my dreams have taken a miraculous course as I have traveled across time through my dreams.

Within this final chapter, I give you a country within this universe I but call Heaven on Earth. Life would give me a chance as I was financially able to travel to the lands of my dreams just before the publication of my sacred book. Walk with me through my dreams as I walk upon this sacred land which came within my dreams.

Sacred journey through the mystical land of castles and history had awakened my inner soul. Sacred, I call all journeys of life, physical and spiritual. Do you believe in dreams? Within my dreams, an unknown country and historical facts related to this country had come to life. Dreams given to me from the unknown come walking into my life within the known chapters of my life.

I walked through this amazing country where the daylight was striking back with all the glows of reality. The places I had visited, the rivers I had seen, the land, the castles, it was as if I was living through my dreams. People from the past were talking to me through the voices of a tour guide. I listened to historical facts of a country I had witnessed within my dreams and now I was walking with strange people from all over the world, taking a tour of my dream diaries.

I had seen dreams of faraway castles, of ruins, and of a very sacred city where the government rules and yet it is not the capital of the country. I had seen the past lives of this country within my dreams. Each time as dawn broke open, I had Googled and found my dreams to be facts of this country, yet from times past. I must say I have seen the future of this country yet walking in front of me too. I had these dreams haunt me. I asked myself why was I being shown historical facts of a country I am not related to?

Some parts of the Netherlands lie below sea level. Yet, she stands tall with historical castles and rolling fields of tulips where windmills are but singing sweet tunes throughout history. The land is ruled by a kind-hearted King and his kind-hearted Queen. The Queen, an immigrant, stands as an example of this great country which accepts differences as a cultural achievement. This Queen shall remain as an example throughout time and history of this great nation.

After reading about this Queen, I felt proud to have known even in these times and days, we have kind-hearted people who are just humans first.

I walked through churches, castles, and buildings and thought yes, historically they were not wonders of this world, but within my soul, they were wonders from history. As I walked through the historical castles, I remembered my dreams of the witches being burned for being different, and the floods of the villages where men had gone fishing. I walked through the castles of the Netherlands and realized so much history is buried within these walls.

I walked and thought to myself if only the past could come to life and walk in front of us. Life that was so vibrant and living, is but lost within these walls. If only we could freeze time, I thought then we could visit the past. Life is a blessing filled with obstacles we all learn from as we move on. I thought of a strange dream where I had left my baby son with a knight as my husband was missing. I had asked this stranger to take care of my baby. All I remember is he had said he would go to Rotterdam near the fisherman's village.

I walked through Rotterdam. The whole city is a miracle to watch the historic churches and the new buildings standing next to each other. The marketplace I enjoyed the most as I got to see the people firsthand. I saw all different cultures walking peacefully next to each other. I met and gathered with the locals walking through this open market, a world market as they carry goods from all parts of this world.

I walked into Grote of Sint-Laurenskerk and was astonished with how much I was attracted to this building. As I finished walking around the marketplace, I just walked into this building without knowing about her existence or what she was. Old buildings pull me to them. I was awestruck with the architecture of the building as she pulled me within her. There were huge statues of The Holy Archangels and all Biblical figures. I spent almost half a day inside and outside the building, walking all around.

I noticed how the Grote of Sint-Laurenskerk goes unnoticed, yet she stands tall with all her historical past as she is the only late Gothic building left in Rotterdam from the Medieval Times. Rotterdam has so much to give, and I loved the diversity of this place.

I knew this land is proud of her history and she is a proud mother as she has taken within her chest all race, color, and religion. Do stop by this great city and take a tour through her churches, the port, and go to the local markets. Try the local food out for then you will see how kind the Dutch are and how they had respected a vegetarian like me. They went out of their way to find good vegetarian food for me to try out.

In addition to riding the tram, and train, I had also taken a local cab to Utrecht which is the birthplace of King Willem-Alexander. Kasteel De Haar as they refer to her in Dutch, dates back to the 1300s and is the largest castle in the country. I walked through this castle as my dreams flashed back. I had walked through a castle, different it may be, but also in the Netherlands, where a knight had helped an unknown person and given her his word of honor.

I was shocked as I walked within Kasteel De Haar. There was a knight on top of a tower which I took as a sign. Even though I did not see a real knight, it was nice to see a statue of a knight on top of the castle. I felt good that maybe not physically, but spiritually, the knight from my dream was somewhere within this country. The tour guide had mentioned this castle was known to be haunted or maybe still is. Interestingly, within the Knight's Hall, they had installed hooks on the ceiling to catch the ghosts of the past, or maybe knights, roaming around still to this day.

Binnenhof, in Den Haag or The Hague, is a miracle. This is where all the politicians gather and work. Yet, this is so open to all the citizens. I walked within the historical buildings and had my dreams come alive in front of me. I watched the courtyard and had known this place from years of dreams of the water fountain, the square where all the news crews gather, and The Plein behind Binnenhof where tents are placed and people sit through rain or shine. Even if you are in the Netherlands for a day, do go visit this place. Have coffee and sit and enjoy the international crowd.

If not a vegetarian, do try the fish at the entrance of Binnenhof. The crowd is a proof of their popularity. They were so kind and so many people had offered to make different things for me.

Each person on this Earth has a miracle to speak of and that is the wonder of life. History can't speak alone, but through the lives of the past. Yet, so many stories have not made history, but remain in the memories and are passed on through the words of the wise through generation after generation.

I believe somehow, somewhere, the buildings, trees, skies, and rivers of this Earth all have a sacred chest where they store all the hidden stories of the past. Life is lost from our eyes, but the tree that was planted hundreds of years ago still weeps for her owner as she carries the memories of all the past owners. She stores all the stories of the past within her soul.

Throughout time, we recollect them sometimes through memories, sometimes through dreams. Dreams are the true wonders of this Earth as they stand within the eyes of the beholders and Mother Earth dignifies each one of these dreams as she brings them out to reality throughout time. Buildings, churches, and castles with so much dignity and character from the past still exist within the Netherlands. Ghost stories haunt the streets of Amsterdam. Today, tourists from all over come to Amsterdam, the home of the Anne Frank Museum. The old buildings, churches, and castles even talk throughout the dark nights of their past inhabitants. Witches still exist through the memories of the inhabitants as houses still have dream catchers and hooks to get rid of evil souls. Storytellers are all walking around with so many stories to share with all the visitors, yet as I walked within the earth of this beautiful country, I knew so many stories have been lost within the pages of history.

Still standing in Oudewater is the famous Heksenwaag, also known as the Witches' Weighhouse where the poor women were saved from being executed as they were falsely accused of being witches. This weighing house was within my dreams. The weighing scales still exist for all who want to weigh themselves, hoping maybe they too have some magical powers of a witch. Yesteryears, the poor women were terrified of being a witch and today I know there are so many who want some powers, some magical healing powers.

I give my honor to this country as throughout Europe and America, we live with the knowledge of executing the accused witches, yet this land had given freedom to these witches at this weighing house. People accused of being witches, from throughout Europe, had come to this land to escape the brutal execution and have a fair trial.

I walked through this sacred country and knew Mother Earth had wanted me to visit her, for I had a dream the same night I had landed upon this country. I saw Mother Earth in the form of a beautiful woman. I cried and told her I am an orphan as I have no one on this Earth and I feel so lost at times.

I felt tears flowing from my eyes as I saw mothers cuddling their children and being there without being judgmental or criticizing, but just being there. Mother Earth held my hands and told me to know if she is here, I will never be an orphan. She told me in her sweet voice, "I am Mother Earth and this Earth you stand upon is my chest, my soul. These oceans that flow from land to land are but my tears trying to unite all of my children on Earth."

I was within the warm comforts of Mother Earth and I knew I would be just fine as I have my faith and love of my Lord within the walks of my life. The skies poured almost every day I was there on my blessed trip. I knew the rain was a sign of blessings from the Heavens above.

I wanted to stay at a place far away from all the hassles of a tourist city. I also wanted to avoid Amsterdam as within my dreams, I had been there on a honeymoon and been at a hotel which was not even renovated during the time I had the dream in 2012. Years later, this hotel had a grand opening and so did the Dunkin' Donuts from my dream. Yet, I had seen both the hotel and the donut store in 2012.

I walked into the hotel and swallowed the painful memories of my dream. The building, the surrounding, all were standing in front of me. Also, were with me a few friends whom I had shared this dream with in 2012. They were all in a shock as to how all of this is possible. I don't know the answer as still the man from my honeymoon is missing and I don't know when or how I will meet him, but I have faith.

I stayed in Rijswijk, a few minutes away from The Hague. I found a small boutique hotel called "Restaurant, Hotel & Spa Savarin." I must say this was the best place I had stayed in my life. The murals on the bedroom walls are paintings from the School of Hague. This hotel also has a past written all over her walls, which had made this stay even more amazing.

Do touch the walls of all old buildings as you visit them and remember someone from the past had also touched these walls. The only bridges in between the two of you are the walls and time. I loved it even more than the great Caribbean vacations I had taken in my life.

I felt like I was in a place of peace and serenity. The crew and the guests alike were very special and made me feel normal, not like I was having a once in a lifetime vacation. I was peacefully awakened and had the feeling of real people, real soul, not a stage where you put up a show and don't remember the audience as you leave the stage. It was a serene, peaceful environment for families and couples alike.

Yes, true it is also a spa and you could get all the luxury of being treated at the spa. I, however, avoided the spa as I just wanted to spend my time with Mother Earth and walk upon the soil of this blessed country.

I had let my Lord guide me to the places to visit and be during my stay in the Netherlands. I had visited Amsterdam, Rotterdam, castles and museums, the windmills, and the canal boats. I had traveled by tram and the rail as this beautiful nation is connected through great transportation. I was lucky to be at the market which happens on a Tuesday in Rotterdam, and the final bazaar for the season in The Hague which was held on Sunday, the last day of my trip.

I love to go to local bazaars and craft shows as this is the only way you get to meet the local people, and get connected to their culture. The Dutch have great knowledge of different languages and speak great English. They are kind-hearted, warm people who don't show their feelings, but are generous and warm. I was told from the tour guides that the Dutch do not show their feelings and are very reserved, and do not hug or talk much, so to just be polite and all shall be fine. I have had different experiences as I talked with the restaurant waiters, the passengers on the tram, and all people in the bazaars.

I spoke with the police and security all over this land and each individual person was so helpful and kind-hearted, I was shocked and amazed at their personalities. Every single person went out of his or her way to help a stranger. The sales clerk at the ticket booth for public transportation spent so much of her time helping me out. She had handwritten all the names and places, spelling out the pronunciation in English so I would understand. Do try out the public transportation. It is amazing and all the passengers love to help if they realize you are having a hard time understanding the stops and locations. I had hugged and was given so many hugs from all ages of people. I felt like I was living with my family and friends. I still am in touch with so many strangers whom I now call my friends.

Throughout my life, I have been fortunate to travel throughout this great Earth and fall in love with all different race and culture. I must say though, I felt my eyes betrayed me as I felt tears fall when I had said my farewell to this great nation. I cried like I had left my long-lost love behind and it hurt so much. I felt a strange bond with this land. I walked through the stories of the witches, the knights, and the long-lost love stories whispering through the windmills, the fisherman's village where the floods had struck, and the castles standing tall. Peace is a word I felt completely within the lands of this spiritual country.

I will, however, talk about one city, one town, one place which took my breath away. I feel like if on Earth, I could call one place Heaven on Earth, in my eyes, within my soul I felt it was Den Haag, or The Hague in English. This was such a peaceful place as I walked throughout the city center. I had walked to the Peace Palace and knew it was not just this building, but this whole city should be called peace on Earth. I did tie a ribbon on the wishing tree and prayed for all human race to be in peace and find peace as we be the first to spread peace to be in peace.

After traveling through India, the Himalayas, through Australia, the Caribbean, through the Americas, I landed upon this small country and I feel I have found Heaven on Earth.

Where is Heaven on Earth? If you ask me to answer this question, I would say wherever you find peace, complete peace, is your Heaven. In my eyes, within my soul, I found peace knowing a country I had visited within my dreams does exist. All the visions of this unique country that I had witnessed within my dreams, allowing me to travel time and see her past, present, and future match today's reality as she stands. This is a miracle and for this miracle, this is my complete inner peace and my Paradise found on Earth.

My Heaven on Earth is where the past teaches the present through history. Through the windows of the past, we the present feel the presence of our past generations. This city has kept all the windows of the past open to the present generation, be it good or bad, the stories are alive each day throughout this town.

I call this country, a country on bicycles, with family bicycles that have covered children and pet sitting areas. I have seen auto rickshaws in India where you hire a man to drive for you. After the ride, you live with guilt as to how you could let an old man drive you around. In this country, you have people carrying their own loads for themselves.

Den Haag is a small boutique like city, where historical buildings stand tall, talking from the past. The old buildings, the courtyards with fountains and sundials, dream catchers spread out throughout to catch all bad dreams and the evil spirits of the past. I call this town an authentic antique town where the buildings and the past talk and represent an authentic antique village where all the politicians and citizens walk on the same path.

I brought back within my soul an art of an antique village where all the people and buildings stand tall like a storybook village. It is the only land on Earth where the government is so available to the citizens and to the children all the time. The buildings stand tall with so much history of pain, sorrow, and love stories. One could feel the ghosts of the past just watching over their future generations with so much love, and wisdom.

History teaches us from the past even when all is lost within the wheels of time, life lives on within the pages of history. The buildings have withstood all the obstacles of time. Life has moved on and today different generations, different cultures, and different races walk upon these courtyards listening to the tales of the yesteryears. Today, the government of this beautiful country sits here, so openly walking amongst the public.

I saw within this complex, ministers walk chatting with children and adults, and answering all different questions being raised to them. So open is this nation. I know why the children of this nation are called the happiest children in the world. They have the blessings of their past generations, for the past even today teaches the present through the tales of the past. The present listening to the stories of the past knows what to do and avoid. The wise have said do not say, but listen and be the wise. I walked through the Binnenhof and knew not only was it a blessed journey for me through time, but it is always standing tall for the future generations too.

I have been to all different continents of this Earth and found out all in their own ways have a gift for this one world we share. The Netherlands is a small country with so much wealth of history and love that she shares with her citizens and us the guests whom she treats with love and tenderness. I call her a great and kind hostess you don't want to leave behind, yet bring back within your soul all the kindness, love, and wisdom she blossoms throughout her land.

I left this land with so much tears within my soul. When I finally came home, all my friends have asked if I left someone behind. Did I finally fall in love, and was I bewitched by a stranger who took everything from my soul and left me with only memories from the past? I answered no, not yet. One day maybe, but for now yes, I did fall in love with a stranger I call the Netherlands. If this country was a handsome, available man, then I would give all my love to him. For now, I must say I have fallen for a country, I call the motherland of all Dutch.

I told them maybe even if she does not adopt this American child, this American child has adopted her as a mother within my soul. If this is love, then all my friends, yes, I have fallen deeply in love with a nation, a faraway land that comes and blesses me within my dreams. I guess love comes at the strangest of times and I have fallen for a country that I had no clue of, but now I know she has and always will have a special place within my soul. For all of you who live there, all my blessings and for all of you who have not yet made it there, do make some time within your travels to visit her.

Stand upon this blessed land and feel the magical touch of eternal peace and love of this blessed country awaken you from within. For me, I feel awakened within my sacred, spiritual soul. If a land could do magic, I know it is this blessed land called the Netherlands. Blessings pour from the Heavens above, as we capture and spread them across the lands, the oceans, and the skies.

I have spread all my blessings across this land from within my dreams. Visit her once within your lifetime and I know you too shall share this blessed dream.

As I was en route back to Seattle, I just had a feeling I wanted to say my goodbyes. I posted on Instagram, "En route to Seattle, will be home soon, yet I miss the Netherlands already." Immediately, I was shocked to get a reply from Schiphol Airport, "Have a good flight! We'll miss you too." I keep these words sacredly within my soul until we meet again.

With all my love and blessings, I dedicate my seventh book, *Spiritual Lighthouse: The Dream Diaries Of Ann Marie Ruby* to the Netherlands.

I am not naming this chapter as she completes my entire book. For this reason, I have decided to call this chapter, "The Final Chapter."

FROM WITHIN THE SPIRITUAL LIGHTHOUSE[10]

My Lord, my Creator,

This sacred soul but seeks solace

Within my mind, body, and soul.

My soul walks the path of present, past, and future in search

Of peace and solace, my Lord.

This soul has wondered throughout sacred words

Of the wise philosophers, my Lord.

I have walked within the blessed books

Of all religious houses, my Lord.

I but have walked throughout the paths

Of Your devoted scientific scholars, my Lord.

From dawn through dusk,

I worship only You, my Lord.

From this dark night as dawn is yet to break open,

I kneel only to You, my Lord.

Guide this soul to shore as I but ask, seek, and knock,

For peace and solace, my Lord.

I find peace as I know,

My Lord guides from The Heavens above and Earth beneath.

With hands held up high,

My Lord The Omnipotent,

---

[10] Exclusively written for *Spiritual Lighthouse: The Dream Diaries of Ann Marie Ruby*

Catches from within the dark ocean, one by one,

All the lost and stranded children.

Guiding, protecting, and blessing eternally is but my Lord,

The Omnipotent, The Omniscience,

FROM WITHIN THE SPIRITUAL LIGHTHOUSE.

ABOUT THE AUTHOR

I am an unknown person who lived the struggles, overcame the obstacles, as I have endured the pain and joy of life as they landed upon my door.

I like to be the unknown face to whom all can relate. I want you to see your face in the mirror when you search for me, not mine. For if it is my face in the mirror, then my friend you see a stranger. The unknown face is there so you see only yourself, your struggles, your achievements as you cross the journey of life. I want to be the face of a white, black, and brown, as well as the love we are always searching eternally for. If this world would have allowed, I would have distributed all of my books, to you with my own hands as a gift and a message from a friend. I have taken pen to paper to spread peace throughout this Earth. My sacred soul has found peace within herself. May I through my words bring peace and solace within your soul.

You have my name and know I will always be there for anyone who seeks me. You can follow me @AnnahMariahRuby on Twitter, Ann Marie on my personal Facebook profile where the username is /annah.mariah.735, @TheAnnMarieRuby on my Facebook page, ann_marie_ruby on Instagram, and @TheAnnMarieRuby on Pinterest.

For more information about any one of my books, please visit my website www.annmarieruby.com.

I have published four books of original inspirational quotations:

Spiritual Travelers: Life's Journey From The Past To The Present For The Future

Spiritual Messages: From A Bottle

Spiritual Journey: Life's Eternal Blessings

Spiritual Inspirations: Sacred Words Of Wisdom

For all of you whom have requested my complete inspirational quotations, now I have for all of you, my complete ark of inspiration, I but call:

Spiritual Ark: The Enchanted Journey Of Timeless Quotations.

I have also published a book of original prayers:

Spiritual Songs: Letters From My Chest.

Now I give you my seventh book:

Spiritual Lighthouse: The Dream Diaries Of Ann Marie Ruby.

MY SPIRITUAL COLLECTION

Spiritual Travelers:
Life's Journey From
The Past To The
Present For The
Future

Spiritual Messages:
From A Bottle

Spiritual Journey:
Life's Eternal
Blessings

Spiritual Inspirations: Sacred Words Of Wisdom

Spiritual Ark: The Enchanted Journey Of Timeless Quotations

Spiritual Songs: Letters From My Chest

Spiritual Lighthouse: The Dream Diaries of Ann Marie Ruby

BIBLIOGRAPHY

Al-Bukhari, Muhammed Ibn Ismaiel. *Sahih Bukhari*. Web. 27
    November 2017. <https://www.sahih-
    bukhari.com/Pages/Bukhari_9_87.php>.

"Berakhot." *Sefaria.org*. Web. 27 November 2017.
    <https://www.sefaria.org/Berakhot.55b.1?ven=Tractate_Be
    rakot_by_A._Cohen,_Cambridge_University_Press,_1921
    &lang=en&with=Versions&lang2=en>.

"Dreams." *The Oxford Dictionary of Islam*. Ed. John L. Esposito.
    Oxford Islamic Studies Online. Web. 27 November 2017.
    <http://www.oxfordislamicstudies.com/article/opr/t125/e55
    7>.

Jung, Carl G. *Man and His Symbols*. London: Picador, 1978. Print.

Jung, Carl G. *Memories, Dreams, Reflections*. Ed. Aniela Jaffe.
    Trans. Clara Winston and Richard Winston. New York:
    Vintage Books, 1989. Print.

King James Version. Bible Gateway. Web. 27 November 2017.
    <www.biblegateway.com>.

"Mandukya Upanishad – 12 Verses on AUM." Web. 27
    November 2017. <tripurashakti.com/mandukya-upanishad-
    12-verses-on-aum/>.

Prabhupāda, A. C. Bhaktivedanta Swami. *Bhagavad-Gītā as it is.*
Bhaktivedanta Book Trust, 1989. Print.

"Qabbalah Page." The Nazarenes of Mount Carmel. Web. 27
November 2017. <essene.com/B'nai-Amen/qabbal.htm/>.

"Sotah." *Sefaria.org.* Web. 27 November 2017.
<https://www.sefaria.org/Sotah.2a.9?ven=Sefaria_
Community_Translation&lang=en&with=all&lang2=en>.